Barely Breathing

10 Secrets to Surviving

Loss of Your Child

DAPHNE BACH GREER

Foreword by

TODD NIGRO

Barely Breathing
10 Secrets to Surviving Loss of a Child – 1st ed.
Daphne Bach Greer
www.AlyBlueMedia.com

Cover Design by Strubel Studios, LLC
Interior Design by AlyBlue Media LLC
Author photo by Angel Feathers Photography
Published by AlyBlue Media, LLC

ISBN: 978-1-950712-03-8
AlyBlue Media, LLC
Ferndale, WA 98248
www.AlyBlueMedia.com

This book is designed to provide informative narrations to readers. It is sold with the understanding that the writers, authors or publisher is not engaged to render any type of psychological, legal, or any other kind of professional advice. The content is the sole expression and opinion of the authors and writers. No warranties or guarantees are expressed or implied by the choice to include any of the content in this book. Neither the publisher nor the author or writers shall be liable for any physical, psychological, emotional, financial, or commercial damages including but not limited to special, incidental, consequential or other damages. Our views and rights are the same: You are responsible for your own choices, actions and results.

PRINTED IN THE UNITED STATES OF AMERICA

TESTIMONIALS

Daphne draws from the depths of her own painful loss to share some very practical secrets to assist grieving parents in finding their moorings again. She helps readers see that though life will never be the same again, peace, hope, and even joy are still possible through a vibrant relationship with Jesus Christ. This is recommended reading for any parent who is grieving the loss of a precious child. —JILL SULLIVAN, While We're Waiting Ministry to Bereaved Parents co-founder

Barely Breathing offers an honest, uplifting perspective that touches the heart and offers hope to those who have suffered the loss of a child. Daphne's faith through the grieving process enables each reader to see the possibilities beyond the seemingly impossible task of learning how to live one's life again after such a great loss. —HEATHER WALLACE-REY, author of Faith, Grief and Pass the Chocolate Pudding and Grief Diaries: Surviving Loss of a Parent

A book this powerful could only have been written by someone with a living testimony of recovery and faith. Daphne's writing is real and unfiltered, exposing the unexplainable pain of losing a child, while sharing her deep compassion and love for those searching desperately for healing that seems impossible. Every path, every journey through grief is unique, but in this book, Daphne shares her secrets, the individual steps she took on her own journey, that led to the only path that ends in life and hope. This is a book that could be read over and over again, each time relevant to your present walk through grief." —PASTOR LANCE & QUINN PRUETT, Glen Ellen Community Church, Glen Ellen, California

Grief is universal and non-linear, yet that can be so hard to remember when you're in it. However, Daphne Greer speaks to those who are suffering like a friend by your side, reminding you to just breathe with each tidal wave of pain that will hit you without mercy. Barely Breathing is truly a light to those who are suffering in the deep, dark depths of grief. Greer's profound understanding of what grieving entails, language used, and the format of this book serves as a vital roadmap for grievers wherever they may be on their own journey. She leads her readers through her own story of the loss of her daughter, Lydia with compassion, grace and genuine care—leaving you feeling inspired and hopeful. Her ten secrets that everyone in grief should know were thoughtfully written and easy to follow, all while being real with the ever-present reality that loss never goes away, but rather it becomes a part of us, pushing us to grow in ways we never saw coming. As a mother myself to a child who has passed, every word written was relatable, thought-provoking and left me with a breath of fresh air—a grief book that is absolutely for everyone. —LINDSAY GIBSON, author of Just Be: How My Stillborn Son Taught Me to Surrender

DEDICATION

To my darling daughter Lydia.
My firstborn, keeper of my heart,
may your light always shine.

And to the many grieving parents
today and those coming tomorrow,
may you feel God's comfort and hope
through your darkness. Trust and know
He is with you always, and so am I.

CONTENTS

Barely Breathing

BY TODD NIGRO

FOREWORD

Life is like an ocean. For forty-two years I felt like I was traveling along in a speedboat. It seemed as though the meaning of life was to zip from here to there on the best boat. I was determined to provide my family with a life full of exciting opportunities, and we zoomed from one activity to the next.

My boat was a success and I was in control. I maneuvered around obstacles and went where I wanted, even though it seemed as though we always needed a better boat.

But, where were we going?

One day, that boat crashed in spectacular fashion when our family's youngest sailor was killed in a home accident. It felt like our family was now adrift, floating separately from one another in the water. We needed help.

The waves crashed upon me as I gasped for air. I was not in control.

It became obvious in those moments that there was help. God was right there. I asked Him to take the helm. In that moment, He sent me an empty rowboat. I climbed in and asked God to help us.

He assured me our youngest was with Him, and then took charge. Together we located the rest of my family and pulled each one into His rowboat.

In the early days, we saw many boats zooming past as they went from here to there, much like we had prior to the home accident. We also saw many boats crash, throwing people into the water. A few seasoned sailors purposefully guided their boats next to us, and shared stories about their own crashes, the storms they endured, and how to find hope and purpose in the aftermath.

Although life felt like an ocean, in reality, on January 20, 2012, our sweet six-year-old daughter Ellie was killed in a tragic home accident. As one would expect, this resulted in months of shock, bouts of depression, insomnia, anxiety, memory loss, difficulty relating to friends and family, weight fluctuations, and so much more.

But there were seasoned sailors who made a difference. They took the time to reach out and listen. They provided encouragement and strength because they had survived and found a way to serve others. I was contacted by a bereaved father who shared his tragic story, his testimony of hope, and what he learned on his journey. A bereaved mother and widow reached out while still healing from her own serious injuries and let us know that we can find our way through this.

Sleeping was difficult for me. I read many books and articles in the evening. One night I came across Daphne Greer's blog, Grieving Gumdrops, and was intrigued. As I read her words, I found hope and inspiration.

A year later, as our nonprofit Ellie's Way began to grow, I asked Daphne to write an article for us. Daphne has been a huge supporter ever since, and volunteers as one of our administrators in the Ellie's Way Group, a large online support group on Facebook.

Daphne has a heart of service and compassion, despite her circumstances. Her story and words of wisdom have brought me great comfort. Daphne is shining a giant beacon of light into the dark valley of grief with this book.

Thank you, Daphne, for giving us this gift.

TODD NIGRO

Ellie's dad and founder of Ellie's Way

What do you say? There really are no words for that. There really aren't. Somebody tries to say, "I'm sorry, I'm so sorry." Sorry doesn't do it. I think you should just hug people and mop their floor or something.
~ Toni Morrison

INTRODUCTION

The quote above perfectly describes the heart of most grieving parents. There are absolutely no words to say when a child dies.

If you're reading this book, I am very sorry. No one should ever have to read this book. Unfortunately, we become involuntarily initiated into this horrible club. It's a place of debilitating pain and sorrow so deep, I never knew it existed. Yet strangely, this rupture of our heart also can become a place where compassion blooms and hope is ignited.

As a parent, most never imagine needing to read a book about child loss. Just the mere thought about having your child die is sheer terror. For me, it was something I never considered until about three weeks before our car accident. Coming home from shopping, my mother and I began talking about another family whose child died. Instantly it gave me chills as we confessed how terrible it would be.

Yet, moments later we returned to our safe, cozy, and normal lives, not giving it a second thought. Little did we know that we would be in this same situation days later.

At thirty-one, I was confident and strong. I held the world by the reins, believing I could conquer anything. I was a working wife and mom with a challenging yet exciting career in law enforcement. Who would have imagined that a routine drive to work on a beautiful summer day would change the course of my life?

It was early in the morning, July 16, 2008. My daughter, son and I loaded up in our red little commuter car and headed out to daycare. With both children securely buckled in their seats, we pulled out of the driveway and were on our way. As we approached the stop sign at the end of our street, five-year-old Lydia, in a bold, loud statement cried, "But I didn't get to tell Daddy I love him! Turn around!"

Really? Do we have to turn around? She is so bossy. Why is she doing this? She's never done this before. Why today?

"Can't we just call him on the way?" I asked.

"No!" she exclaimed. I didn't want to be late for work, but how could I possibly disregard such a heartfelt plea? She loved her dad, making the term "Daddy's girl" an understatement.

With my heart leading the way, I turned the car around and we met my husband, Jake, in the driveway just before he left for work. She jumped out of the car, ran to her dad with arms open wide, smiled sweetly, and in her squeaky, charming little voice said, "I love you,

Daddy." Lydia literally gave him the hug of a lifetime. Skipping happily back to our car, she hopped in and once again we were on our way.

Just a few short minutes later, after saying goodbye and telling her daddy she loved him, my healthy and vivacious firstborn girl on the verge of entering kindergarten, would leave this earth.

The accident happened in the blink of an eye. Just seconds before, my little darling was brushing her strawberry blonde hair in the backseat as she sang her favorite tune from the movie Annie, "The Sun Will Come Out Tomorrow."

And then.

The deafening sounds of clashing metal, screeching tires, and a young child's screams haunted me for years. They are sounds I'll never forget.

What just happened? I did my best to stop in time, but it wasn't enough. I sat in the ditch among the tumbleweeds and gravel, clinging to my three-year-old son and waiting for help as my daughter lay lifeless in her car seat.

My life flashed before my eyes. It was an accident, but what had I done?

Days after the accident, I looked into the mirror and didn't recognize the woman staring back. She was a stranger. Who was I? A terrible mother? All sense of identity and normalcy was stripped away, leaving me just a shell of a person with nothing left inside.

The thought of drinking myself into oblivion to escape my new reality, I have to admit, was very appealing, however I was terribly fearful I would lose control and wouldn't be able to stop.

After my daughter died, you could say the world ended. It was that simple. My life had come to the lowest point you could ever imagine. I was surrounded by complete darkness. There was no purpose, no meaning left, so why continue living? She was only five. Suddenly, nothing mattered anymore. I had failed. Failed to protect my most precious gift. Failed horribly as a mother. I was at the bottom of the food chain. My future had been destroyed, or so I believed. And now, for the rest of my life, I will be a grieving mother. A frightening thought and a tough pill to swallow.

Imprisoned by guilt, I lived in the blackness, the far back corner of my closet, shielded by my hanging clothes, which offered a strange sense of security. It was there, where no one could see or hear me, that I released buckets of tears and drowned in my emotions.

Such a tragedy didn't happen to people like me. I was living the American dream complete with a magnificent husband, two beautiful children and we both had challenging yet amazing careers in law enforcement. Our life was what others only dreamed of. Yet sadly, I didn't comprehend the value of what I really had.

It doesn't take long for us bereaved parents to realize that our life has become strictly about survival. Survival, as defined by Merriam-Webster, is to "continue to live or exist after...tragedy or difficulty." We are never prepared for the emptiness that awaits.

Surviving child loss is about pondering our existence and re-learning those basic needs and principles of life. Learning to eat again. Learning to take care of yourself again. Learning how to communicate again. Learning how to live this life that you don't want live without your child in it. It's a horribly frightening and fragile situation, and at first you see no way out as your mind frantically tries to make sense of the senseless.

We have now begun walking this earth with fragmented hearts, pierced by endless shrapnel when those difficult moments arrive. It's an ache that never goes away. Deeply wounded, it's a pain so excruciating that we plead and bargain to trade places with our children, desperate for anything to relieve us of the misery we are going through.

The loss of a child transports us to a place where we feel trapped, unable to escape as we teeter between fantasy and reality, because this could not possibly happen to us. We instantly become older and wiser, receiving a doctorate in something we never imagined.

As for me, I've always been the strong one in both my immediate and extended family. I wasn't afraid to speak my mind, and said what others were thinking but didn't have the courage to say. The one who acted. The one who held it all together.

Yet when my daughter died, I lost it all. I didn't know what being strong meant, nor did I care. I wasn't strong, yet I felt I had to be strong for others. How twisted was that?

I remember all the people who came to visit shortly after Lydia died and me carrying on, having conversations about everything except my daughter. Engaged in superficial banter, somehow trying to comfort others and responding to their condolences of, "I'm so sorry," by replying, "That's okay." What in the world?

It wasn't okay.

I wasn't okay.

Yet here I was telling them what they wanted to hear. Can you say ridiculous?! The things shock and grief do to us. All we want is someone to sit with us and listen, gifting us a temporary moment away from the sheer loneness that grief encompasses.

I scoured the internet and libraries for books offering proof that I could survive. There is nothing worse than thinking about the future without your child by your side.

It was very hard to read books the first year. Bits and pieces I took in stride. Little by little I digested what I could and ignored the rest. Some information I wasn't ready to hear and that's okay. I didn't need to hear it then. Please don't rush yourself. Take all the time you need.

But I am here to tell you I survived this and am living a joy-filled life, and you can too. However, I'm not going to sugarcoat it. Burying your child or children is the most unbearable pain you could ever imagine. You will cry, you will scream. Heck, you may even throw things as you crumble to the floor in disbelief and fear.

This goes on for days. Weeks. Years.

At times, it feels like we're drowning in the sorrow. When Lydia died, I was desperate for an immediate fix. Unfortunately, there's no medicine to fix this, no practical solution. No *Grief for Dummies* or *Cliff Notes* for how to survive. No fairy dust or magic potion to make our child return. Believe me, I searched the earth for it. We bereaved parents want to run and hide because the grief is so paralyzing.

Important dates come and go, and milestones and benchmarks become our new normal, whatever that is.

When we realize our children have been gone longer than they were here with us, we sink our heads in disbelief.

When our friends experience high points in life that our children never will, a sucker punch blindsides us. It's painful and it sucks, and there's nothing we can do about it.

Yet, through all these trials and milestones and all the "firsts" we experience without our child, I'm here to tell you some secrets to help you survive this nightmare.

But first, who are we kidding? We absolutely cannot handle this on our own. We need to engage the help of everybody we know, but most importantly our heavenly father.

Whether you believe in God or not, the death of your child is the biggest thing you'll ever go through in your entire life. And trust me, it's nothing you can do by yourself. I don't care who you are. Celebrity, athlete, preacher, teacher, doctor, or the world's strongest man—you can't do this on your own, yet that's nothing to be ashamed of.

They say it takes a village to raise a child. Well, it takes a village to mend a broken heart as well.

We as humans are weak and not meant to fight battles alone. That is why He is here. Give your burdens to the Lord. It may sound easier than it is, however, let me tell you there is power in His name. This is not just some crazy nonsense I dreamed up. It's real. I know. I've experienced it and felt it. Only through Him can our souls ever be satisfied and make us stop searching for that peace and contentment that eludes us. We must have constant reminders of who we are and where we came from.

But more importantly, I am here to tell you that you can survive this and you are never alone. Never.

Whether you are newly bereaved or have been struggling with loss for years, I want to share what has helped me. I have written my ten secrets to survival plus some bonus secrets for you. I want all those parents out there with aching hearts to know that there is hope and that if I can do this, so can you.

How do parents whose child has died, move forward when they don't know what do to next? How can we live this life when reality tugs back because the fear of moving forward is so gut-wrenching and hard? What do we do when we feel like we can't take one step further and we want nothing more than to be with our children? When our horrendous wails terrify us because we've never heard ourselves utter such noise? Let's face it—our hopes and dreams have been shattered.

We feel like outcasts, like we don't belong anymore because the only identity we have ever known has been stripped away in a second. As already said, there are no words. However, what I can offer is some hope and encouragement, while planting seeds of faith.

The transformation from deep grief to a hope and peace-filled life does not happen overnight. The transformation of the heart and soul is a work of God. Molded and mended over time, He can slowly heal us, though our scars will remain forever.

The strength of a grieving parent is enormous. We are forced to create a place where life is real and pain is palpable, yet hope and faith dominate. Differences are washed away and we are transformed into superheroes without even being aware. God holds us up.

We live like no one else. Our fragile hearts are burst wide open, teeming with compassion. Along our journey, we may become weak and our faith is tested. However, by turning to the word, we can be rejuvenated with the infectious persona of faith in Christ. Eventually, we will learn to live differently holding our child's love in our hearts.

As time moves forward, equipped with the armor of God to sustain us and protect us, we can be refreshed and renewed, filled with hope and healing. He is the only way. He alone provides freedom from the shackles of grief and sorrow.

> And now, dear brothers and sisters,
> we want you to know what will happen to
> the believers who have died so you will not
> grieve like people who have no hope
> (1 Thessalonians 4:13).

Hope is essential. God wants us to cling to that hope He has instilled in us.

Certainly some of these secrets I am going to share with you may not be viable until some time has passed. It may take months or years before you're ready to conquer some of the secrets because, as we know, the journey of a grieving parent lasts a lifetime. The pain will come and go, be unbearable at times, yet tolerable other times. Such a strange dance.

So here are some treasures found, to help you navigate this world of unfathomable sorrow, from one grieving parent to another.

Together we got this. Beautifully broken, and yet united.

We are stronger together.

DAPHNE GREER

Lydia's mom

Remember to breathe. It is after all,
the secret of life. ~ Gregory Maguire

SECRET 1

BREATHE

After you learn your child has died, the only thing you can do is to breathe. Or try to breathe.

Our bodies are screaming and shock takes up residence. It hurts. The shortness of breath makes us feel like we've just ran a marathon, when we took really only a few steps.

Every ounce of our being is telling us we need to run away from this torturous reality. If only we could.

We wonder how we're even still alive. Inhaling and exhaling feels heavy and laborious. Our mind tricks us into thinking we're physically ill, and we just may be. But the majority of the time, it's anxiety and shock coupled with a broken heart.

My body and self became out of sync after Lydia died. As evening neared on July 16, 2008, I remember being in the hospital, watching my husband kneel beside my bed and tell me my daughter had died. I remember the screams and gut-wrenching wails that poured from my body. Disbelief overtook me.

Ten hours later, with my arm wrapped in a sling and bandages on my forehead, I was pushed out of the hospital in a wheelchair dressed in a gray sweat suit. A white bag holding my belongings hung on the back of the chair. Lulled by medication, I was dazed and confused. My mind teetered between reality and fantasy. I was barely breathing.

My advice to you, amidst the tears and heavy grief, is to breathe and take things as they come, one minute and one day at a time.

The first day, night, weeks, and months after Lydia died, it was physically hard to breathe. Getting up for a drink of water seemed like way too much effort. Those first few weeks, I felt exhausted and could barely move from the couch. I even went to the doctor thinking something was seriously wrong due to my shortness of breath. Come to find out, it was just the stress and anxiety of a grieving mother. How sad. Who knew there was such a thing?

It may silly, but many of us don't really know how to breathe or know exactly what breathing does for our bodies. I didn't know there was a specific or proper way to breathe, nor that I had a problem until my daughter's death. Something that always came naturally, I had taken for granted.

Over the years, I grew accustomed to living with that constricted, heavy feeling in my chest, enduring the hyperventilating episodes and panic attacks. Learning to combat those attacks with prayer, they became part of the new me.

Grief is hard on the body both physically and emotionally. Now ten years later, I am a huge advocate for learning breathing techniques. This can make all the difference in the world, and affect your physical well-being during grief.

Rapid shallow breathing is what gets us in to trouble. Our hearts begin to race, thinking of the tragedy and anxiety of the unknown future in front of us. Slowing down, we can regain the calm in our core and steady ourselves. We don't know what tomorrow will bring, so concentrate on today. One day at a time.

When you get nervous or feel panicky, like you can't catch your breath, focus on your breathing. Notice how it feels when you inhale and exhale slowly, in through your nose and out through your mouth.

By learning calming techniques and how to regulate your breathing, you can control this and really impact your life. Sounds strange, but it's true.

Learning how to breathe all over again literally took all my energy. All too often I would find myself forgetting to breathe as I became light-headed and dizzy at the smallest movements. Sounds crazy but I seriously had to make a conscious effort and remind myself to take in that beloved oxygen!

I suffered from extreme anxiety for years after Lydia died. Little did I know that anxiety affected breathing. It had been nearly two years since Lydia went to heaven. While at work one afternoon, I felt my face get flushed, my heart began racing and panic was emerging. I didn't know what to do or why it chose to hit me at this certain time. I couldn't breathe. I walked outside to get some fresh air, but felt light-headed and nearly passed out. I went back inside, walked into my friend's office and, after taking one glance at me, she kindly offered to take me to the doctor.

Long story short, I just needed to talk about it, and release the anxiety. When I began to focus on my breathing, I regained control.

It's incredibly important to take deep breaths. It helps to ease your anxieties and calm the soul. If this was all I could concentrate on and accomplish during a day, I soon learned that it was okay.

When we are struck with such trauma from our loss, day-to-day tasks feel nearly impossible. And you know what? It's okay to let the house go. The heaping piles of laundry, stacks of dirty dishes, unpaid bills, filthy bathrooms, the overgrown lawn, and even the garbage will wait. It's okay, normal, and it happens to the best of us. Just let it go and focus on every breath. Once we have this down, the rest will come in time.

Remember, take it one day at a time. You can do this!

Grief knits two hearts in closer bonds than
happiness ever can; and common sufferings
are far stronger links than common joys.
~ Alphonse de Lamartine

SECRET 2

CONNECT WITH OTHERS

When we lose a child, we become physically and emotionally weak. Connecting with others provides a heart salve that helps mend the soul. My next secret to survival is to make connections with others who have lost a child, for they are the only ones who truly know this horrific journey. This is crucial. Make it a must-do.

Grief is incredibly lonely and isolating. As for any loss, connecting and meeting with those who have similar losses can be life-changing. Your family and friends may not understand. You are different now, and not the same person they once knew and loved.

Friends old and new might now see you as unapproachable and frightening, not understanding why you've changed so much. Months and years can go by, and we hear the subtle words and conversational undertones, "It's time to move on. You should be over it by now," among others. You may not get invited to the social gatherings as they tire of hearing of your sadness. You see, they yearn for their friend back. The old, fun, happy person, but it is one they will not find. It can be a dreadful realization to them. They don't know what to do, and neither do you. Friendships are dynamic and ever-changing. Some become stronger while others drift away.

At the time my daughter died, it was 2008. I wasn't connected to others on Facebook nor the internet. I didn't have it available in my home, nor did I want to. However, my childhood friend who had lost a son three years earlier coerced me into joining the social media giant in 2011, and what did I find? A goldmine for online support groups for grief and child loss. There were so many it was overwhelming. However, I found them and joined some.

At first, reading heartbreaking stories of others who have felt this pain, suffered and endured the loss of their child, was devastating. I found that I wasn't able to read them for very long without becoming anxious, crying and being subjected to heavy bouts of insomnia. I learned to read stories about other parents and their losses in small segments, a few minutes here and there, enough to validate my feelings and be done for the day.

Online support is such a blessing; however, it's also important to have those face-to-face connections with others as well. At the time, I had never heard of child loss support groups, oblivious to the sorrowful reality many others have endured.

The chaplains who stood by our side handed me a brochure from a child loss support group. It had only been three weeks since Lydia died, and my husband had to pretty much drag me kicking and screaming to my first group. I wasn't one to reach out and was a complete introvert at the time, rarely moving from the brown couch that became my best friend.

Nonetheless, we went to a Compassionate Friends meeting. I had never heard of this organization, nor did I want to learn about it. The meeting was in large building attached to the fire department. Opening the door, my hand trembled as it touched the handle. With a quick glance of the room, it appeared to be enormous and filled with people. My husband and I took our seats as the meeting was about to start. I was bitter, angry, and frustrated. It had only been three weeks. I could barely function or talk to people, let alone leave my house, and I was expected to sit through a meeting with strangers? Right!

Reluctantly, I went and hated every minute of it, never wanting to go back. During this first meeting, I sat with my head hung low crying incessantly hoping no one would look at me. Overcome with disbelief and shock, it felt like I was living in someone else's life, not my own. Who wanted to hear about all the depressing stories of grief, seeing firsthand the pain and agony so many are suffering from? Not me. I couldn't even handle my own.

Men and women both young and old went around the table introducing themselves, sharing stories of their children. Staring at the floor, unable to look up, the tears flowed again as I silently wept.

Was I really in a support group for parents who had lost children? Seriously? I didn't belong there, and I wasn't about to speak in front of anyone. Suddenly, all eyes were upon me. Sobbing, shaking, and trying to catch my breath, I muttered, "My name is Daphne and my daughter Lydia brought me here." I thought to myself, how did I get here? This wasn't possible. Was I dreaming again? Someone please wake me from this nightmare! I couldn't wait to get out of there.

But I went back. Weeks later, something drew me to them. Was it the inviting hugs and genuine concern of those seasoned in grief and further down this agonizing path? I wasn't one to ever talk, as I barely muttered my name the first meeting amidst all the tears.

Yet before I knew it, I felt a strange connection. I could relate and soon felt a craving to be near these people, to be able to share my daughter and my journey while joining with others who get it. Our eyes met, our souls connected. A time of quiet solace and reflection. Parents who understand—those who have walked the path. Strangely, at the time there wasn't anything else that brought me comfort.

Here were all these people—old, young, married, single—who had walked my path, and they were still here. Some were barely holding it together, while others paved the way with strength and hope.

This was a group who got it. They understood what it was like to have a birthday or anniversary come around and have no one mention your child's name. They knew the anguish of sitting in the dark alone, crying hysterically on the floor until you had nothing left. They, too, had experienced the loneliness and pain of a home that was now quiet, void of all smiles, arguments and giggles. They understood how it felt to have life stripped away, leaving you without a reason to live. They especially knew how deep my love was for my child.

It was a place where I didn't need to speak, yet found an instant connection with other parents the moment our eyes made contact. Oddly, it comforted my heart to be surrounded by other parents who knew the extreme depths of my pain. They understood. They had all walked in the same shoes. They knew what it was like to hear those words, "Your child has died."

In all honesty, seeing some of these people five, ten, twenty years out from losing a child kind of frightened me. It also brought an odd sense of comfort. If they could do it, maybe I could too.

Unexpectedly, upon leaving the meeting I found myself entering a world of people who didn't get it. Through no fault of their own, they simply hadn't been there. I'm sorry, but there's no way to fully understand it unless you've been there.

When you're feeling disconnected, and are surrounded by others who just can't understand, even though it can be difficult, make the effort to reach out to others who have been there. Trust me. It will bring you comfort in knowing and seeing that you can do this, to see that others have gone before you and survived. You will encounter those who are just a few days or weeks into their grief, and others who are decades out from loss. Each one offers their own encouragement and wisdom.

Of course, you also need your own time—time to process, to feel, to grieve and sort out the whirlwind of emotions. Time just to mourn and release those tears in the safety of your own environment.

It was hard for me to fathom being a member of this club. I struggled with who I was and where I fit in anymore. Where our family fit in. I wanted desperately to find someone who knew what I was going through.

I spent late nights searching the internet, searching for hope, for someone who had survived what I had. There were categories of loss, such as loss to illness, suicide, drunk driver, infant and baby loss. Everywhere I turned was a roadblock and there was nothing for me. No category of "Mom driving car when her child died, no alcohol, drugs or crime involved." I was alone.

Was I the only one? I really only wanted to connect with someone who had been in my shoes, thinking that would make me feel better, but I couldn't find it. Years later I would come to understand that it didn't really matter how our children died. They were gone. We all feel alone, are hurting just the same, and are in this together.

Ten years later, some of these people I have met who have also suffered losses remain my closest friends. They absolutely came into my life for a reason at just the right time.

Let's consider some ways you can connect with others who share similar losses. Where can you find others, a safe sanctuary to talk about your child, or laugh or cry? Aside from close friends, let Google be your best friend. Facebook, too. There are a plethora of support groups and grief groups for parents. There are probably local groups in your area, too. Don't be afraid or ashamed. Reach out. You just can't beat face-to-face gatherings with other parents who know your pain.

Search for local meetings in your town, too, or contact your local hospice for ideas. Here are a few of my favorite bereaved parents support groups in person and on Facebook.

- Ellie's Way
- The Compassionate Friends
- While We're Waiting
- Grieving Mothers
- Grieving Dads
- Grieving Parents Support Network
- A Bed for My Heart
- Bereaved Parents of the USA
- Grief Diaries
- Grief Share

Barely Breathing

"I'll lend to you for a little time, A child of
mine," God said, "For you to love while she
lives And mourn for when she's dead."

"It may be six or seven years Or twenty-two or
three, But will you till I call her back,
take care of her for me?"

"She'll bring her charms to gladden
you and should her stay be brief,
you'll have these precious memories
to comfort you through grief."

"I cannot promise she will stay since all from
earth return. But there are lessons taught down
there I want this child to learn."

"I've looked this world over, In my search
for teachers true. In the crowds of this
great land, I have selected you."

"Now will you give her all your love not
think the labor vain, nor hate me when I come to
call to take her back again?"

It seems to me I heard them say, "Dear Lord, thy
will be done. For all the joys a child shall bring,
The risk of grief we'll run."

"We'll shelter her with tenderness, We'll love her
while we may, And for the happiness
we've known forever grateful stay."

"And should the angels call for her much sooner
than we've planned, we'll brave the bitter grief
that comes and try to understand."

By Edgar Guest

22

Grief is a normal and natural response
to loss. It is originally an unlearned feeling
process. Keeping grief inside increases
your pain. ~ Ann Grant

SECRET 3

JOURNAL

Writing can be an integral part of the grieving process for many. I found it extremely beneficial to keep a journal. Early grief can bring shock, racing thoughts, insomnia and the inability to settle down. What can you do? Start writing.

Put those anxious and fearful thoughts to paper. As grieving parents, we must find healthy ways to purge our bottled up emotions, letting the tears fall—releasing love and hurt as we purge our most intimate feelings.

Writing may not be natural for some, and that's okay. There is no right or wrong way to journal. Also, there is no right or wrong time to begin. It can be immediately after your loss, or months or years later. It's entirely up to you and what feels right. You may write for a few days and then not again for months.

Journaling can be a private healing tool as well. Encouraged by my counselor about a month after Lydia died, I bought a journal.

Nothing fancy, just one from the dollar store. This was a foreign act for me and I wasn't really comfortable doing it at first, writing to my daughter in heaven. It felt strange, frightening and just totally weird, not to mention it produced a river of emotions I wasn't ready to face every time I began.

Months later, a driving force pushed and urged me to write down the path I was taking. I picked up my pen. Feeling terrified and afraid of forgetting, my first entries were memories of Lydia. I put to paper my thoughts, feelings, anything and everything that came to mind. Every fleeting notion was written inside a sacred notebook.

Hesitant at first, I started with simple words on sticky notes, and writing down rushing thoughts I didn't want to forget. These then progressed to a few sentences and scriptures, which ultimately turned into journaling, blogging, and books.

I encourage you to write down your deepest thoughts, and those things you don't want to forget. Record or journal your child's favorite things, moments that made you laugh, everything you miss, the sadness and anger. Try to write it all down.

Write letters to your child. Write down their physical attributes like the freckles on their nose, the boogers on their bedroom wall (that's my girl), their sassy attitudes, love of sports or music, and how they made you smile. Include their artwork or precious mementos. You may even want to color and draw in your journal.

Write down your dreams, too. When I dream of Lydia, I write it down as soon as I wake, before I forget the dream. Those times are seldom, so when they come, we don't want to forget their precious visits from heaven.

Ten years later after reading what I wrote in those early days, I clearly see a picture of light and understanding, and it added a whole new dimension of life. Without a doubt I recommend this to everyone dealing with loss. You just can't recognize the value of your thoughts on paper until years later. I promise you won't regret this!

You may keep your writing private or share it when you feel the time is right. Looking back over the years of my own journaling, I see the dark and painful place I was in, and how it gradually evolved. Below are a few of my early entries.

January 29, 2009

Dear Lydia,

Today is Hunter's birthday. He is four. I remember your fourth birthday. Mom stayed home from work and Grandpa John was here and Papa came over and it snowed all day. You and Hunter played in the snow and we pulled you guys on the old wooden sled. We made a snowman and took your picture hugging the big guy. You were so excited. It was a wonderful day. Today Hunter wanted to know if you could come down from heaven and see him for his birthday. He wanted a Spiderman candle and also wanted a princess candle for you on his cake. Daddy bought the candles and we lighted them on fire and Hunter blew them out, and I put them in the drawer. It was nice but very sad because you should be here with us. I know you are but in a different way. Not a day goes by that I don't think of you a million times. I love you and miss you so much. The pain of losing you seems so unbearable at times and many days it feels like I'm in a dream and any minute I will wake up. I love you and miss you more than anything. You were the best daughter a mother could have. You were so full of life, love and sunshine. You were always so happy. I only wish I would have spent more time with you. I tried to be the best mom and if I could do it all over again, I wouldn't miss a minute of spending time with you. I want to hug and hold you and never let go.

I love you, Lydia.

May 14, 2009

Last night I had a dream about you. It was so real I didn't want it to end. I had to wake you up and you were all sweaty and warm, just like you always were when you woke up. I hugged you and decided to spend the day with you instead of going elsewhere. If only I could have that chance again.

I miss you so bad every day. I see little girls your age and I am reminded of how fun and beautiful you were. I'm going to have the baby on Tuesday and would give anything for you to be there. I know and remember how much you wanted to be a big sister to more siblings. You would always ask for more brothers and sisters. You were the best big sister to Hunter. He loves you so much. He watched your Barbie Island Princess movie the other day because he said he was going to watch it for you. He sang the parts of song the prince sang and I longed for you to sing the princess parts just like old times. Hunter wants to wear your blue bathrobe and talks about you often. Today I picked him up at Kelli's and he and Emma were talking about how much they missed you. Hunter said that God was taking very good care of you.

I remember last summer when you painted my and Aunt Meredith's fingernails. Pink with blue dots in the middle. I put so much clear polish on them to try to make them last forever. A few days ago, I was sitting on the couch and felt something and found one of the fingernails that fell off of my hand so long ago. I smiled and cried at the same time when I saw the pink shell with the blue dot in the middle.

Hunter picked dandelions in the yard for you and wants to bring them to you at the cemetery. I still can't believe you're gone. I feel terrible and it feels somedays like you were just here yesterday. Other days it feels like forever ago. I love you Lydia forever. You will always be my little girl. I will always be your mom.

Three years after Lydia passed away . . .

November 6, 2011

Last night, I got to hold you and hug you tightly in my dreams. It was so real, so wonderful. I dreamt that you had been at Kelli's all this time and she and Nana kept it a secret for me and I went there and saw you through the window. I ran inside and gave you the biggest hug and kiss. You were just like normal, nothing had changed, not hurt in any way. You had shoulder length beautiful blonde hair in a modern cut. You had the same sweet smile. We took you home and had bunk beds for you. Oh I miss you so much. It still hurts so badly. I love you. I wish I could have stayed in that dream forever.

I can't believe you are eight years old and almost nine. It just seems like yesterday when you were a little baby. I am so thankful that I got to know you and spend five and a half great years with you. You changed my life.

November 17, 2011

I sit in my car outside the grocery store right now. It's dark outside and I headed to the store to get milk. I just had to get out of the house. I am tired, stressed, and full of anxiety. I don't know why this is happening. I have no down time. No time to process and no time to spend with you. I am tired of being strong all the time. I just want alone time. Time to sit and think about you.

Your birthday is a week away and you will be nine. It seems the past few weeks I am surrounded everywhere I go by little girls. Girls your age. People talk to me about their daughters who are nine and what they are doing, problems they are causing, fun things and stories about them. I just smile and listen politely while I am crying inside. They have no idea what it's like or what's going through my mind. Christmas is nearing. I was at lunch today with some ladies at work. They were talking about decorating their homes for the holidays and asked if we put up decorations. I didn't have the heart to tell them what holidays are like at my house. Empty and lonely.

August 5, 2018

I found you singing in your room with your pink microphone, ever so softly and sweetly. Of course you were dressed in pigtails and mismatched clothes. "Lydia?" I said in disbelief. "Is it you?"

You glanced at me with that sweet little smile and those piercing blue eyes. It really was you.

With tears streaming down my cheeks, I ran and picked you up in my arms squeezing you so tightly. You were beautiful. I got to hear your voice. Something I was so afraid of forgetting. Blonde hair and pigtails, you looked just like before. Soft skin, adorable giggles. Your Strawberry Shortcake pillow was there too, laying in my closet, just the like the matching blanket I have on the bed.

You never left the bedroom, so I rushed out to get your brother so he could see you once again, hoping you wouldn't leave. Grabbing him by the hand, we ran back to you. As we entered the room, you smiled so big and continued singing, with your great grandma sitting next to you. You were both smiling and laughing—clearly full of joy. Oh I love you so much sweet pea. And then, I kept hearing: "I am alive. Just believe. I'm always here."

If you aren't sure how to get started journaling, visit my website and download the Barely Breathing Workbook for some fabulous writing prompts from my friends at Sent From Heaven.

This should be the motto for every follower
of Jesus Christ: Never stop praying, no
matter how dark and hopeless
it may seem. ~ Billy Graham

SECRET 4

GIVE IT TO GOD

My fourth secret to survival after my daughter died was giving it all to God. All the horrendous hurt and sorrow, the tears, fear, anger and hopelessness. This was absolutely the most important, and essential key to my survival.

I consider myself a tough chick. Strength emanated from my bones. Always has. I've been the one who could always care of herself, change her own tires, navigate the wilderness, and stand up for herself no matter what the situation. I've been one who solves all her own problems, independent and confident. Yet, when my daughter died suddenly, that girl disappeared and I lost all control.

This was bigger than me. I had arrived at a place where life and mortality suddenly became real, awakening me to a surreal world I had facetiously viewed from the outside my entire life. Now, as I was forced inside, I had no answer—no fix, and was submerged in total devastation. There were no words.

We all have these pieces of advice and tools being thrown at us from all directions to help solve our problem—grief and the loss of our children. But our problem isn't solvable. As one of my compassionate friends once said, "You can't replace what you can't replace."

So true.

The problem we have is a severely broken heart, and that can't be solved by a how-to lesson. It's disheartening that everyone wants to try to fix this situation for you, as grief is so uncomfortable for society. I have found that people flounder in their own misery, and rarely mention the power of faith.

There is so much information out there on faith and religion, some supporting and others denying. However, we cannot rely on that secondhand information. We must reach out and grab the truth for ourselves. Around the world there are millions of unbelievers, yet there are millions of believers too.

Then you will know the truth, and the truth
will set you free (John 8:32).

It's absolutely true that the only one confirmed way to receive healing from the loss of a child is through God. Confront this giant by turning to the truth in the word of God. The one and only Bible. The one and only Jesus Christ. We must dive in head first, read it, breathe it, and believe it. And what can it hurt to those who don't believe? Let's plant those seeds and nurture them with love.

Immediately, I knew I couldn't survive this. Not without God. I was alone, my daughter was dead, life as I knew it had ended, and it terrified me. I've been there. I've done medication, counseling, and support groups. I've tried everything to alleviate the pain. And yes, they are inherently valuable and serve a purpose. However, the only thing that can bring back joy and peace was Him.

We can search and search, take pills upon pills, yet only God can provide true healing and hope.

When grief is fresh and raw, it's easy to become angry with God, questioning his mere existence. We wonder over and over again why He took our loved one, trying to make sense of the senseless. We seek answers to life's most complicated problems. Although it's not easy, in order to avoid a vicious circle of torment, we must learn trust and have faith and remember God is the only one in control.

And for me, obsessed with controlling everything in my life, I can say that Lydia's death awakened my eyes to the spiritual world, leaving me thirsting for more.

But let's get real. Faith isn't easy. I've sat with those living with depleted faith, those grappling with anger at an unknown god, wavering between what is real, those demanding proof, and those unbelievers, which is completely normal and common.

So what is faith is and how do we get it?

Let's be honest. Faith is not something you can run to the grocery store to pick up. Granted, that would be pretty convenient. When we're feeling down, we could simply ask a friend to make a pit stop at the minimart to bring us some, wouldn't that solve all our problems? If only it were that easy. Faith can be defined in the Bible.

Now faith is the assurance of things hoped
for, the conviction of things not seen
(Hebrews 11:1).

Essentially, faith is having trust in something you cannot see or prove. Some find it challenging to believe in something you can't see or hold in your hand, and too often, we as humans rely on that hard core slap in your face kind of evidence.

Well, I've also sat with believers. I've gained perspective. If we believe, what have we go to lose? It can't get any worse than losing a child. Why not go all in and see what happens, trusting in the word and finding that everlasting hope that we will be reunited with our loved ones again in heaven? Sign me up! What an amazing day that will be!

After the accident, guilt was a daily burden for me. I wondered, was God punishing me? Had I been disciplined for all my wrong doings in life? Had he kept a list and this was the end for me? Was this the life I was destined to live, in agony and despair, worry and fear, paralyzed the rest of my life? Surely not.

I wondered, why did I survive this? Why couldn't I have died instead of her? After all I had been through, how was it possible to continue living? Why did a child have to die?

I was an absolute train wreck, self-propagating my own demise. Desperate, I had no other choice than to dive into God's word seeking out his promises and the truth. He became my lifeline.

So how does one find such faith? Many of us, yet not all, were fortunate enough to grow up with those seeds of faith and hope, planted at a tender young age. This was true for me. During my childhood, my brother and I grew up going to church every Sunday with our parents, attending vacation bible school, confirmation and participating in all the usual church functions. This was great for my younger years. However, when I moved onto high school and college, my attendance waned as I became absorbed with selfishness, putting my own needs first.

I always needed God and knew He was there, and yet I didn't pay attention to him.

Did I talk with him? No.

Read the Bible? Not really.

My life was good—busy with college, parties, friends and social engagements. I didn't have a worry.

I guess I really didn't need Him back then, or so I thought. He became more of an imaginary figure who lived in the clouds. Regrettably, I didn't give Him a second thought.

That is until the greatest storm of my life swept me into a life of tragedy and sorrow. As too many of you know, there is no bigger test of faith as when your child dies.

When we lose our children, our mortality comes to the forefront and our life suddenly becomes real. In my early days of grief after my daughter Lydia died, I had no choice but to cling to the only hope I had. I had to reconnect with God, to find that reassurance of His love and hope. Desperate and alone, my Bible became my best friend as no one could understand the intense suffering I was enduring.

No one. Not my mother, my father, my brother nor my closest friends. Because grief is unique to us all. It was the one time in my life where I felt completely alone. And it was terrifying.

Nighttime, I buried myself under the covers. I clutched my Bible while sobbing uncontrollably, which provided enough comfort at the time to get a few minutes of intermittent sleep which I was desperate for. I begged God to take me, as the burden of grief was too heavy. Being separated from my daughter was unfathomably frightening which caused me to hyperventilate, knowing there was nothing I could do to return her to my arms.

How does a parent deal with such a torturous reality, seeing that empty bed at night, their daughter's bright clothes scattered across her room, her Barbies, makeup, and artwork all over the house?

How could life go on? Where was God? Did I still believe? How could He let this happen? Questioning everything, somehow I still knew He was real. For the first time, I felt the pain Jesus' mother, and even God himself, must have felt, and knew that although I may struggle to find Him, see Him, that he was there, somewhere.

For a long time, I grappled over why I had survived the accident and Lydia didn't. She was only five. Having no explanation for this caused me to live with suffocating guilt and condemnation. It haunted me, told me I was worthless and deserved nothing. My faith was full of questions.

Feeling helpless and hopeless, I deliberated why I should continue on in life. How exactly does one go on after such a loss?

I began reading the word of God firsthand. I quickly learned He would not let something happen without creating something more beautiful to bloom after. After all, God is love and He wants us to receive his unconditional love.

Yet, it was not enough. We as humans, sit and replay the past and question everything. Why me? He must not love me. What did I do to deserve this? Why, Why?

My soul was tired, leaving me no choice but to surrender control. I had always retained control of everything in my life and suddenly I had none. I desperately craved it.

As humans, we don't understand tragedy. We see it every day, but don't believe it will ever happen to us. Yet, no one is immune.

Up to that point I had been one of the lucky ones who had the luxury of living without turmoil. I had it all—the American dream, a husband and two children, and a fulfilling career. Then one morning it was taken from me in a split second. What did we have then? Where was God? Who was God? Was there a God?

Those days of hopelessness and darkness hovered over, weighing me down. Panic set in. I began searching, desperate for a flicker of light, a glimmer of hope, yet all I could feel was the bitter coldness of the world. For months, I scoured the internet for stories and books about angels, miracles and heaven. I needed to know how we got there, what heaven looked like, whether Lydia was alright, and who God really was. I needed proof, or so I thought.

> Therefore we are always confident and know that as long as we are at home in the body we are away from the Lord. For we live by faith, not by sight. We are confident, I say, and would prefer to be away from the body and at home with the Lord. So we make it our goal to please him, whether we are at home in the body or away from it
> (2 Corinthians 5:6-9).

I soon found what I needed to know. Finding peace that my sweet Lydia was there, resting eternally and present with the Lord brought me a sense of comfort.

> And I heard a loud voice from the throne saying, "Look! God's dwelling place is now among the people, and he will dwell with them. They will be his people, and God himself will be with them and be their God. He will wipe every tear from their eyes. There will be no more death or mourning or crying or pain, for the old order of things has passed away" (Revelation 21:3-4).

I had to know the Lord better. I needed to find out more about Him because this was bigger than I. However, looking back, all I really needed was Him. Why had I not done this before? Why had I placed Jesus in my pocket, to leave him there all those years ago?

Through my searching, I discovered this longing to be closer to God. Even though those evil and detrimental thoughts telling me to satisfy my aching heart, to be with her surely would alleviate the pain. I knew He was my only hope and my only way out of this turmoil.

> The Lord is near to the brokenhearted and
> saves the crushed in spirit (Psalm 34:18).

My faith provided a sense of comfort that nothing else could. Not that I had any clue how to read my Bible or amass knowledge of its powerful contents, but I knew it held those few shimmers of hope that I needed. Those few verses that I held tightly, carried me.

What did I have to lose? Nothing, because I felt as if I had already lost it all.

> Jesus answered, "It is written:
> Man shall not live on bread alone,
> but on every word that comes from
> the mouth of God" (Matthews 4:4).

Well, there it is.

This was the absolute reassurance that I needed. We can't live on food and water, we can't live on what society and the world tells us, but we can live and are to live on every word that comes from the mouth of God. I needed someone to tell me it would be okay, that I would survive. That I would enjoy life once again. But no one could.

Rejoice in our sufferings, knowing that
suffering produces endurance, and
endurance produces character, and character
produces hope, and hope does not put us to
shame, because God's love has been poured
into our hearts through the Holy Spirit who
has been given to us (Romans 5:3-5).

So I began to pray. I didn't really know how to, so did it my own way. A few words here and there, crying, whispering, shouting, pleading, you name it. I prayed and believed in the power of His word.

Be joyful in hope, patient in affliction,
faithful in prayer (Romans 12:12).

Praying for God's hand in everything. Getting through one day at a time. Praying for healing in my marriage, praying to help me control my finances, praying for God to make those flashbacks subside, praying for forgiveness and wisdom to learn how to forgive others, praying to learn how to love again. Praying to be able to learn to love myself again and open my fragile heart to love others despite the risks of losing them.

The challenge is to place complete confidence in Him and understand that God is with us throughout our suffering. To believe that we are never alone, and he wants us to rely on Him through the good times and the bad times. And that we shouldn't wait, we should praise him now in the delightful times as well as the rough times.

Our life is not meaningless. He created each of us with a plan in mind and a purpose to fulfill.

The shallow faith I had been living in previous years made me realize how incredibly superficial I was. It's quite embarrassing now looking back.

I casually attended church when convenient, rarely opened my Bible, and was easily annoyed by bible thumpers and those who played Christian radio stations in their work cars. I mocked and criticized them. In retrospect, I am deeply ashamed of my past behavior.

It was a time in my life where I thought I didn't need God. I had it all under control. Boy was I wrong.

Over the years I have found it's not for us to know the whys. But it is our job to trust. To believe and receive His peace amidst our struggles. He is there. His presence is all around us.

It's simple. Without faith, we have nothing. This life on earth is so short compared to the eternal life that awaits us. Faith is not based on evidence or proof, but on truth and belief in what you cannot see.

Faith is a gift from God. He has to be enough. I've felt the deepest pain possible, and I'm a living testimony that He is enough. However, if you are not ready for God, He will wait for you. Understand, that it often takes our hearts breaking wide open before Jesus can come in.

Keep pressing on. Keep seeking the Lord. You have nothing to lose. You can do this!

> I can do all things through Him who
> gives me strength (Philippians 4:13).

"If you have tasted of Hell, you cling to the Lord of heaven," Sheila Walsh stated in her book *The Shelter of God's Promises*. Isn't that the truth?!

So what are you waiting for? To get started, take a few minutes each day alone to find God. Purchase a Bible if you don't have one, look online, at the library or your nearest church. His powerful words are everywhere, just waiting to encourage and uplift you.

> Your most profound and intimate
> experiences of worship will likely be in your
> darkest days—when your heart is broken,
> when you feel abandoned, when you're out of
> options, when the pain is great—and you
> turn to God alone. ~ RICK WARREN

Grief is like the ocean; it comes on waves ebbing and flowing. Sometimes the water is calm, and sometimes it is overwhelming. All we can do is learn to swim. ~ Vicki Harrison

SECRET 5

READING & OTHER DISTRACTIONS

I never learned to swim, but did learn how to use a lifejacket. I love the above quote as it perfectly depicts the life of a grieving parent. Swim or tread water, just keep your head above the surface.

Here is secret five: Reading and other distractions. Seriously, can we escape this just for one minute? Grief is exhausting. Intermittent distractions can help us survive.

We're not ignoring grief, just putting it aside for a bit to realign and recalibrate ourselves. While we must feel, acknowledge, and work through grief at our own pace and in our own time, we're all different. What works for one might not work for another. We are all unique beings, and handle the trials of life in our own manner.

Grief is scary enough. Grieving your child is utterly terrifying. I believe distractions are necessary to help us cope with such trauma as the loss of a child.

We can't submerge ourselves in sadness all the time, we need a reprieve. We need to come up for air, to catch our breath before we are pulled back down into the dark abyss.

After spending countless nights mastering Super Mario on the Wii with my surviving son, reading soon became my lifeline after Lydia died. Initially, I had to know Lydia was okay. I scoured the internet for books about God, Heaven and the spiritual realm, which were immensely helpful. I needed more and more. This filled me with glimmers of hope.

A good book can make an almost impossible existence, livable. ~ Charles Bukowski

However, one thing I needed was time off from grief, yet its unrelenting hands rarely offer such a break. So, especially at night while overwhelmed with sadness and it was difficult to sleep, I found myself needing an escape.

In addition to self-help books, it is important to read what I call mindless books, the amusing fictional ones that capture our attention. While they may be ridiculously meaningless, they can transport you to a different world, taking you places you've never been.

I soon learned I had to stay away from any book involving death, murder and mystery. But I tore through humorous and entertaining books like a kid through a candy store! From home decorating, to romance, to local history, I left no stone uncovered.

Reading gives us someplace to go when we
have to stay where we are~ Mason Cooley

I desperately desired, especially during those dreaded long nights, to go to a world that was not my reality. It brought relief being able to focus on a fictional story and somehow live that life until I was able to fall asleep. I'm sure I would've won some kind of award for reading the most books in a short amount of time, if there was one. If you're not into reading, there are many other distractions such as painting, coloring, crafting, building, gardening, knitting and other hands-on activities to focus your energy and mind, which can be therapeutic.

Sure, distractions are not the solution to soothe a grieving heart, however, they may help buffer the hurt a bit until you are ready to absorb the pain little by little.

Early on, I tried to keep busy and distracted in the daytime. Nights proved to be extremely difficult for me. Something about the darkness brought my hurt to the forefront. The thought of the sun setting and darkness ensuing horrified me and I dreaded it. I would cry and sob in disbelief. I knew this is when my pain was the greatest. I had to see my girl's bedroom with no light on, no more middle of the night bathroom breaks, no more arguing over bedtime, knowing she wasn't in there. How in the world would I be able to sleep?

When the study of heaven began to cause me amplified sorrow, I indulged myself in mindless reading. Scared and exhausted, I opened my drawer to find a stack of old hand-me-down books from my mom and cousin and started the Shopaholic series, by Sophie Kinsella. Submerging myself into the characters of a fantasy world was just the ticket to temporarily calm the painful burning of my grief. Thank you Sophie! This was just what I needed at just the right time!

Whether it be driving in the car or sitting on the couch at home, it didn't take me long to realize that in those early months, anytime of day when I was alone was the hardest. I kept busy for so many years after Lydia died juggling children, work, and activities that I didn't have time for grief. I guess you could say I intentionally kept myself occupied to soften the sadness as I became a master at avoidance. Yet, in those moments when life stopped, even if just momentarily, my mind would immediately turn to the events of that horrific day she died, and the tears would fall like a torrential rain. But that's okay.

The stillness held me captive, forcing me to remember and to experience the reality of what I was living. I could feel the emptiness as it encroached into my body. Knowing that Lydia would never again walk through that front door was terrorizing. For years, being alone, day or night, made me feel the raw pain and brought me to a place of guilt and sorrow. And it scared me.

As the years continued, slowly my alone time transformed into a peaceful retreat where I was able to process life, its purpose, and replay memories of my beautiful girl. Now, when the sun sets and darkness falls, I may be found shedding silent tears as I fall asleep, leaving black mascara stains on my pillow as evidence of those difficult nights. This was my new normal.

Your heartbreak will always remain as those distractions come to a close, and you won't forget that. However, at times, it does help not to have to live in that deep hole every hour of every day.

When we're grieving, we need the occasional break from our reality, as the mind can only take so much before it overloads. Overcome with grief and trauma, I still look forward to my escapes, giving me some much-needed rest from the heavy weight of my sorrow.

It's not something you will ever get over. It becomes part of the new you. Something you learn to live with over the years, yet at first may be a bit too heavy to carry. That's where distractions come in.

Many people think that keeping busy or distracted isn't the right way to go about grief. However, an important reminder: there is no right way to grieve your child. We all handle loss differently, and that's okay. We must go through grief at our own pace. You'll have sharp painful times when you feel everything, and days when your sadness will lessen and you suddenly realize you are smiling for the first time since your child passed.

Some dive headfirst into work, others travel or start a project. My husband and I decided to tackle our house and build a huge addition. We had never done anything like this before, and while challenging in many aspects, it was a good diversion for us. Regardless, do something that brings you comfort. Go for hikes, see a movie, cook your favorite foods, read a book, start a hobby, join a club, go out to dinner with a friend, plant flowers, go to the beach, exercise, etc.

The only way to do things, is what feels right to you. If you're not an active person who can stay busy or diverted, just do what is comfortable for you. Reminder again, this is only a suggestion.

Distractions can be a well-needed gift to the grieving. We are forever learning to navigate the unknown world of child loss, balancing our two worlds of past and our current unbelievable reality.

So, what can it hurt? In those first years you will have painful milestones and endless triggers that thrust you into an emotional whirlwind. So, celebrate when you feel like celebrating, cry when you feel like crying. No filter, no shame. A break in our grieving ritual just may turn into a new perspective.

Most importantly—don't judge yourself or let anyone else judge you. You are doing just fine. One day at a time. You can do this!

If you know someone who has lost a child,
and you're afraid to mention them because
you think you might make them sad by
reminding them that they died—you're not
reminding them. They didn't forget they died.
What you're reminding them of is that you
remembered that they lived, and that is
a great gift. ~ Elizabeth Edwards

SECRET 6

HONOR YOUR CHILD'S MEMORY

Do we celebrate, remember, recognize, or simply ignore? My sixth secret to surviving the death of a child is to honor their memory. And there are countless ways to do this.

First, let's just get honest and say that it's imperative that you honor your child's memory, birthday, or the date he or she went to heaven. It doesn't matter how, just honor your child. Yes, even this can be a tough one, especially early on as we have no clue what to do when those days arrive. As the months and years pass you will want to do this. I promise. All a grieving parent wants is for their child to be remembered.

After Lydia died, for months I worried and was completely afraid that people would forget her, that I would forget her. The sound of her voice, the smell of her hair, the sprinkle of freckles on her little nose and arm. It was paralyzing, and stirred a fear in me that could not be calmed. What an awful thing for a parent to experience. Of course we want to keep our children with us, every ounce of their being. We want people to talk about them. We want to talk about them. Their belongings, quirks and accomplishments, treasuring those reminders that they lived and that their life mattered.

We want them acknowledged. And it brings joy to our hearts when we hear their names. Even ten years later, I will always want my daughter to be remembered. Our children will forever be our children and we will always be their parents. Nothing can change that. Ever.

Shortly after Lydia died, my husband and I joined a support group for bereaved parents. Uncomfortable at first, as twenty-five grieving adults sat around the table, I listened to stories about how they tackled and acknowledged birthdays and death anniversaries of their children. They exchanged accounts of baking birthday cakes and buying small gifts for their deceased child, and shared other ways of celebrating and reminiscing. For several months I had a difficult time processing this, and thought them to be loony. What could they have to celebrate? Are they crazy? What is wrong with these people? Are they deranged? These thoughts, and many more, raced through my clouded mind.

Anticipating Lydia's birthday that first year without her, I couldn't bear the thought of having a cake. The pain was too great and I believed there was simply nothing to celebrate. How disrespectful of people to do such a thing. When her birthday came only four months after she died and no one acknowledged it, not even my family, I was devastated. I couldn't bear the thought of having to celebrate that day. Clearly, neither could they.

She was the first grandchild, the first granddaughter and anxious for her arrival at birth, everyone welcomed her.

Thanksgiving Day 2008, was Lydia's first birthday in heaven. We had the usual extended holiday gathering that included grandparents, cousins, aunts, uncles, brothers and sisters. With twenty-plus people, we were all there—except Lydia. In years past, it included cake, gifts and a joyful celebration of Lydia since her birthday occasionally fell on Thanksgiving day. But this year was different.

Overcome with emotion, I couldn't eat and felt nauseated as I took my seat at the table. I pushed food gently around my plate with the fork, listened and watched as my family smiled and visited with each other. Thanksgiving? What did I have to be thankful for? Lydia wasn't here. It was her birthday. I wanted to talk about her. I missed her. I would have given anything to be able to hold her again. I wanted to curl up in a ball and sob. I wanted to hear her name and remember my little girl.

I'm sad to say that not one family member mentioned Lydia's birthday. Not one! Did they forget? Were they afraid? The reason didn't matter. It broke my heart and I wondered if it would be like this for the rest of my life. Why couldn't anyone say her name? I knew the answer, but it angered me, and I didn't have room for any more pain.

My family was close, yet lacked effective communication skills. They never touched on subjects that mattered and shied away from anything that involved sensitive matters of the heart. They were treading lightly to avoid causing an uncomfortable atmosphere, but their avoidance of the subject of my precious girl didn't remove any hurt and only weighed me down even more.

Unbelievable. Lydia's first birthday in heaven, six years old, and no one said a word.

My heart was broken and I felt a sense of betrayal. Again. I felt pain on an entirely new level. The void was already there. Lydia was gone. It was as if they pushed the knife in further, adding pressure with a slight twist. I wanted to scream. Didn't they get it? Didn't they have a clue? Did they remember? Were they just uncomfortable? Well, what about me? What about Lydia?

That empty chair at the table, that prolific elephant in the room lurked like a predator in the wild. There was an unspoken silence, an uneasy feeling among the party. Everyone knew it was her birthday, yet no one muttered those words or even mentioned her named. I couldn't wait to leave and retreat to my car so I could shed tears. I was tired. I didn't care about offending anyone or protecting their feelings.

As time passed, my thinking changed. While difficult at first, after two years, the fog slowly cleared and I realized what I was missing out on. The lightbulb had turned on. Of course she should be celebrated! She's my girl. She was so full of life and bursting with personality, and this is what she would have wanted.

Here is my journal entry three years after Lydia went to heaven. The pain is still so sharp when I read this again.

December 1, 2011

Your birthday was three short days ago. No matter how much I want to forget the pain of that day, I can't. No one called. I received two text messages from my two closest friends saying they were thinking of us. Received a text from Jake's sister who said the same. Not one phone call. It was like an unspoken silence. It was devastating that not one family member could call us and acknowledge our daughter's birthday instead of pretending it didn't exist. People seem to think after three years we need to be over it and they move on with their lives but we still remain stuck with nothing but memories. I know that everyone grieves in their own way and many do not know what to do, but really? I cannot tell you how horrible it felt. We spent the day at the carousel with the kids and then went to the shelter to visit our favorite little boy and his mom.

It was then when I understood what my fellow grieving parents were talking about. They are our children. They didn't just vanish, they weren't a figment of our imagination. They were here and they matter. Real, living, breathing souls full of life and love.

Every year since then, my husband and I make sure to honor our little princess by writing messages to her on balloons and releasing them. Silent tears stream down our sorrowful faces as we watch them soar into the blue sky. Along with our other four children, we sit and stare until we cannot see them any longer. We watch in wonder as they disappear into the clouds, pondering life outside this world while remembering our girl.

At the present time, my husband, children and I are about the only ones who recognize Lydia's birthday. Yes, it does hurt when others don't remember, but we can't expect them all too. Some may believe it's too painful for us, or it may be too painful for them, while others believe we should move on and get over it. And really, who cares what other people think? She was here. She lived. And, you know what? She still has a birthday!

It's now been ten years. Yikes! That is still so hard to believe. Every year on Lydia's birthday, we gather as a family, enjoy her favorite meal of chicken strips with french fries and ranch dressing. We take turns exchanging memories and stories of our beautiful girl. We will forever celebrate this beautiful day, the day God blessed us with her, and we are reminded of how our lives have been impacted because she lived.

It wasn't always like this. For years, I wasn't able to eat her favorite dinner or dessert, or even visit places she loved because I was trapped by guilt. This is an ugly monster, but one we can overcome together. Yes, it is possible.

But what about the day they died? The dreadful anniversary date. It wasn't long before I became acquainted with the terminology associated with my new identity. The term "anniversary" took on a whole new meaning. Without a doubt, it can be devastating and difficult as this day approaches every year. Anticipation and anxiety can consume us. A death anniversary? Well, those words are ugly. I prefer to call it the day Lydia went to heaven, as do my friends at While We're Waiting, a refuge for bereaved parents. And what a rejoicing day that was for her.

Honoring and celebrating our children can be a bit scary, and many are apprehensive like I was at first. I wondered what others would think because, as stated previously, my confidence and self-esteem were shot. Like it really mattered.

Lydia's heaven date (anniversary) falls in midsummer. It's a day that's filled with painful memories and immense grief, a day that can't go unrecognized. It's a tragic day that changed our lives, a day I can never forget.

On July 16, you will find us gathered at the cemetery consumed with bittersweet sadness, donned with pink and purple flowers for Lydia. We are riddled with sorrow yet see a glimmer of hope as we picnic at her graveside with her favorite lunch—cantaloupe, chickens strips, french fries and ranch dressing. We proudly celebrate her life, acknowledging the joy and love she brought to each of us.

Honoring and remembering our child also bring opportunities to create new traditions and beginnings we can embrace when the time is right. They can bring comfort and peace, encouragement and hope.

When we were at about the three-year mark, I felt the urge to do something to honor Lydia's memory by helping others. It also served as a reminder that her life mattered, and became a driving force of motivation and an act of outpouring love. With my creativity flowing and in partnership with our church, we created Lydia's Place and Lydia's Love.

Lydia's Place is a cheerful playground, full of bright colors which represented her personality to a T. Purple, pink, yellow, blue, orange and red, complete with multiple slides, monkey bars, and activities, Lydia's Place is still being enjoyed by children in our community. It always brings a smile to my face and fills me with happiness.

With the completion of Lydia's Place, I still wanted to do more. As a result, Lydia's Love, Inc. was created in 2011. A nonprofit organization that provides birthday parties to homeless and needy children. This has been a rewarding and heartfelt experience. Seeing joy in children's lives during hard times, as they feel and know that they are special, is priceless.

Needless to say, honoring and remembering our children fills a void in your heart that nothing else can. I greatly encourage you to ponder how you can celebrate your child. Where there's a will, there's a way. Anything is possible, big or small!

To top it off, I wear a necklace with Lydia's thumbprint and name engraved on the back. It's a precious memento that I've worn for ten years now. Truly the best gift I had been given.

Here are some ideas on ways to remember and honor your child.

- Read their favorite books

- Donate to a charity in their name

- Create a memorial garden at your home

- Wear their favorite perfume, nail polish or cologne

- Make a scrapbook with photos and mementoes

- Plant a tree

- Make a photo quilt or quilt out of their clothing

- Make a teddy bear from their old clothing

- Get a tattoo in memory of them, their handwriting or artwork

- Spend time with family and friends sharing stories about your child

- Start a scholarship program

- Bring flowers to their grave

- Cook their favorite foods

- Listen to their favorite music

- Adopt a part of the highway

- Release balloons or lanterns or butterflies

- Memorial jewelry

I love you every day.
And now I will miss you every day.

~ MITCH ALBOM

> The best way to find yourself is to
> lose yourself in the service of others.
> ~ Mahatma Gandhi

SECRET 7

BRING JOY TO OTHERS

The next secret to surviving the death of my child was bringing joy to others. Nothing is more fulfilling or rewarding than serving others. Whether it be in a small way or a big way, this can heal you like nothing else. From feeding the homeless, to sending a short thank you card, to giving a smile to that one person who may need it most. By making a difference in the life of another human being, you can't help but notice that it will lift your spirits and give you a sense of worth, pride and healing.

Co-founding an organization in memory of my daughter has been an extraordinary experience. Being able to reach out to underprivileged children and see them smile has impacted me and my family in amazing ways. How incredible of God to use Lydia to bring sunshine to those in dark places.

Over the last ten years, I have gained wisdom far beyond my years. I was forced to grow up before my time, facing my fears and tragedies head on. Diving deep into my faith was the only answer. No one could help me or give me the magic potion to fix this pain, despite my longing to do so. My eyes were opened to a whole new world that I never knew existed. I was desperate to fast-forward through this horrifying heartbreak.

Grief. It was real and so very debilitating in the first few years, causing physical ailments and poor self-worth. Yet as time went on, it presented me with an incredible sense of humility and oddly, breathed new life into me.

I was different. Different than before the accident happened, and ever so different to my friends, whom I had known for years. I could care less about the ridiculous and trivial problems my friends often complained about in my presence, steering me toward the company I enjoyed being part of. I now attended support group meetings for bereaved parents—a once foreign land. I found comfort knowing these mothers understood what I was going through.

We gained our strength together by sharing our stories and our children, both the happy and the sad, the good and the bad. They had been there. They got it. They appeared so strong but were also weak like me. And for the first time, I felt a tiny shimmer of hope igniting inside me.

This is where things began to change.

The unselfish effort to bring cheer to others
will be the beginning of a happier life
for ourselves. ~ Helen Keller

It had been eighteen months since Lydia had passed away and I was asked to join the board of my local chapter of The Compassionate Friends. Exploring ways to encourage and support our members, every week I saw new hurting parents join our table, revealing their own loss and heartbreak. Little did I know, this is where my heart would remain for the next five years.

It ignited in me an unyielding passion to serve others, and soon I found myself hosting birthday parties for underprivileged children, feeding the homeless under the bridge and volunteering at church. It was amazing.

> The darker the night, the brighter the stars,
> the deeper the grief, the closer is God!
> ~ Fyodor Dostoyevsky

Before the accident, bringing joy to others wasn't really in my wheelhouse. I hadn't volunteered much before except at my children's school, and in college at the fire department and local prison. What I didn't know is that giving back not only produces a positive impact on others, but it impacts you, by transforming your heart and mind. Any type of volunteering or giving back, helping others and your community, can't help but sow seeds of love and kindness.

Volunteering helps heal my broken heart, bring joy to others, and can help you, too. Let God use that pain!

It helped me take my mind off my own circumstances. Grief is sneaky, it likes to haunt you and keep you feeling down and hopeless.

However, volunteering kept me occupied and made my heart empathize with others going through life challenges, realizing we are all in this together. All the while, it quietly boosted my confidence and stirred up joy that was buried in my heart.

> At the end of the day it's not about what you have or even what you've accomplished... it's about who you've lifted up, who you've made better. It's about what you've given back. ~ Denzel Washington

Here are a few of my thoughts on the benefits of bringing joy to others by volunteering.

Volunteering gives perspective. When we are in the deep throes of hurt and sorrow, we feel like we have experienced the end of the world. In all reality, life could always be worse. Not to diminish the pain and tragedy we all go through, but seeing the struggles of others makes one understand that everyone suffers in life, some more than others and making you thankful for what you do have.

> How many times had I sat next to people who were suffering but been completely unaware of the agony they were going through? ~ Levi Lusko

Volunteering makes you focus on what really matters in life. It can help you view life in an eternal perspective, reaching far beyond this life on earth and help you see where and how you can make a difference. It provides you a sense of your purpose. You are living and doing to make others feel loved. To let them know they matter. From helping feed the homeless to impromptu conversations at the hospital with strangers or in the grocery line, there are others who could use a little hope and encouragement. And you are placed in their path for a reason. Live in awareness and don't miss an opportunity to be a blessing to others.

Volunteering and bringing joy to others unites people. We are passionate beings with tender hearts. It's important for us to emotionally connect with others and let them know they are not alone. Forming new friendships also helps boost your own morale and aids in depleting that feeling of loneliness accompanied by grief. Giving back makes you feel part of something bigger than you.

Volunteering humbles you. It has made me tremendously grateful. Volunteering exposed to me the things in life I had taken for granted while offering me understanding and presented me with a renewed compassion for others. Serving others also provides an opportunity for self-reflection and meaning. With this, I learned to appreciate each new day and all the gifts I had been given in life, realizing that I was not more important that anyone else in life. That we are all equal.

Volunteering is a rewarding venture that provides fulfillment like nothing else. It gives you an internal change. A transformation of the heart. Giving fills a void and satisfies that deep hunger for life hidden inside.

I prayerfully encourage you all to consider where you can make a difference this year, whether in a small way, doing simple acts of kindness or a big way by chasing your dreams. By following through and making a commitment, you will open yourself to incredible life-changing experiences that you won't regret. Give it a try!

And remember......

Those who bring sunshine to the lives of
others cannot keep it from themselves.
~ Mother Teresa

Spread love everywhere you go. Let no one ever come to you without leaving happier. ~ Mother Teresa

Find out where joy resides, and give it a
voice far beyond singing. For to miss the joy
is to miss all. ~ Robert Louis Stevenson

The meaning of life is to find your gift.
The purpose of life is to give it away.
~ William Shakespeare

SECRET 8

FIND A NEW PURPOSE

After such a devastating loss, I was lost. I didn't know who I was anymore, but what I did know was that I wasn't the same person. My life was infinitely different. Experiencing the death of your child is unnatural and changes your identity forever. Finding a new purpose is my next secret to surviving the loss of a child.

For me personally, the struggle with guilt was horrendous, like a heavy weight on my chest, never lifting. Every breath was an intense fight for survival. I couldn't look at myself in the mirror. I was afraid. Afraid of who I might see, and afraid of who I had become. Was I now that mom who caused her daughter's death? Why did I live and not her? The questions consumed me, slowly demoralizing my spirit and leaving me with no self-worth.

I dreaded looking into the mirror for the first time. I didn't know who I was anymore, and scared I might not recognize my own image. Regardless of how I looked, I believed that the only face I would see was that of a terrible mother.

Finally facing the mirror one day, I didn't recognize the woman staring back. She was a stranger.

Who was I? A terrible mother? Was I still a mother? All sense of identity and normalcy was stripped away. I was am empty shell, with nothing left inside.

How do we find ourselves again? How does one rebuild when they don't want to, or don't know how?

Two and a half years later, I found myself searching for a purpose in life. I didn't fit in, and felt useless and hopeless. I was broken and at a standstill. I prayed incessantly, asking God to guide me and give me direction in the path I was to take.

When our child dies we are instantly thrust into a foreign world, not knowing what comes next. Those first few nights which turned to weeks, months and years, were frightful and strenuous. If a bystander had looked in our window as we turned out the lights and lay in bed in the silent darkness, what would they have seen?

They would have seen a mother and father soaked with tears, terrified with another day gone, clutching their surviving child's hands and as well as each other's. Bowing their heads and in their trembling voices, you could hear them quietly asking God for strength to get through another day, to ease their sadness, the courage to be a parent to their only child now, and faith to show them the way.

Seeing the sunrise each morning meant time was moving on, but I wasn't. Over the years, the nightly ritual of pleading prayers turned to thankfulness and praise for the time I did have with Lydia, asking God again to guide us as to our new life and purpose.

God has done amazing things. He has been the foundation in which our marriage and family has endured. Hope became the catalyst to surviving this new life we had been given.

But it hasn't always easy, immediate, nor crystal clear on which direction to take. Does moving forward mean we are forgetting our children or not honoring them? Absolutely not. Does it mean we shouldn't be happy for ourselves? Not at all.

While we ponder these decisions with trepidation, we lack focus and energy. Simply planting those seeds and then meditating on which direction to take, if any, can influence our path.

For example, can or should you change careers? Your focus, or path in life? Definitely. Why not? However, I would recommend not making any drastic changes in the first year, as your rationale may not be the best during this time. However, there is no right or wrong time. We all grieve differently, and are unique in our own situations.

However, I believe that most of us lack the confidence in life to chase our dreams, to actually follow through with what's on our heart. We worry about failing, what people think, and talk ourselves out of it before we even start.

After your child dies, you'll reach a place when you feel ready to move forward (which may take years), and you become determined to live your best life in honor of your child.

It's bizarre, but suddenly your life comes into focus and you realize what matters most. And you come to believe that your child wouldn't want you to live in sorrow and despair the rest of your life.

Having a busy and stressful career as an adult parole officer after Lydia died, I found myself being ineffective at my job. I welcomed my wandering mind, oblivious to what I was being paid to do. My career wasn't for me anymore. My life was different now. None of this mattered. I found a whole new empathy and outlook on life, one that embraced compassion and understanding for others who were also enduring tough times. Slowly, doors began to open while some painfully closed. God was showing me the way.

Losing my daughter opened my eyes to another world, which posed questions. Why are we here? What is the meaning of this life we have been given?

Life is too short not to explore your dreams and passions. So after fifteen years, I ended my career and set off on new adventures. I now volunteer in many organizations, work with the elderly, facilitate self-empowerment groups for at-risk teens, contribute my writing to magazines and books, and help others navigate through the brambles of child loss. In retrospect, it was the best decision of my life. A huge weight was lifted from my shoulders, and I felt a sense of freedom and satisfaction that is hard to describe. I know now my purpose in life is to help others through tragedy and hard times, and to share God's word. It fulfills me and drives my motivation for life.

Please know, it won't always be so painful. There will come a time when you'll find that joy again, whether in a smile, a laugh or a precious memory. And what if we let God use our pain?

For me, finding a new purpose lifted the weight and replaced the emptiness with an exhilarating feeling of freshness, new beginnings, possibilities and hope.

So how do you find your purpose? Try recalibrating your moral compass by listening to your heart, find what brings you joy and gives you peace. Do what feels right. Find your gift. You are brave, so take that leap of faith. You have nothing to lose!

> The strength for your next season will come
> from the pain of your past. Yes, your
> pain has a purpose. ~ Toby Mac

The more passionate you are about
setting your soul to heaven's time zone,
the more progress you will make in your
calling here on earth. ~ Levi Lusko

Only when my eyes have adjusted to the
dark can I witness the splendor of the moon
and stars. Only when I have sat in hopeless
loss can I appreciate every blessing.
~ Angela Yuriko Smith

SECRET 9

GRATITUDE

My next secret to survival after child loss is gratitude. What exactly is gratitude? As defined by Merriam-Webster, gratitude is a feeling of thankfulness. But seriously, how can anyone be thankful after their child is no longer living?

Can grief and gratitude really coincide? Sorrow and joy? The last thing any grieving parent wants to hear is, "Just be grateful for this, that, and whatever."

Seriously, our child just died and nothing will bring them back. Life is forever changed for the worse.

I frequently find myself telling my family and others around me to slowdown in their lives and count those blessings. Blessings? What blessings? That's what I thought in those early days and months, even years after Lydia went to heaven. I dodged those comments, "At least you can have other children, at least this. . . at least that . . ."

How in the world was I blessed? I mean, my firstborn was taken from me and I will never hold her in my arms again.

When you experience child loss, it's difficult to see good things in life. It wasn't until about the third year after she died that I was able to see Lydia's life as a blessing. I missed her so much. God had slowly revealed to me the impact her life had on so many. Now this doesn't mean that I still don't cry myself to sleep or feel the intense pain of my daughter's absence, because I do. I will shed endless tears the rest of my life. As time continues and I see her friends going to proms, getting their driver's license, reaching those milestones that she never will, it still hurts more than ever. All we can do is inhale deeply and let it out slowly. This too will pass.

As bereaved mother and creative artist Franchesca Cox puts is, "When you lose a child, you are haunted by a lifetime of wonder." Isn't that the truth? Losing your child brings a lifetime of sorrow and you suddenly believe that there is no way to continue living. On the other hand, grief can also illuminate your senses, and bring to light everything in life that matters, as well as show you everything that you've previously taken for granted. We grieving parents become proficient at a delicate waltz as we learn to balance the two worlds we live in, remembering the past while embracing the future, experiencing both sadness and joy at the same time.

What if we change our perspective and try to identify the positive things in our lives? Years after Lydia died, I eventually began to use my hindsight to see beyond my loss.

So what if I was tired of the sorrow and heartbreak. What if I decided to look at that glass half full? Did it mean I loved her any less? Did it mean that I didn't miss her or wish she was still here? Did it mean my guilt was magically washed away? Absolutely not. On the contrary, it meant she showed me a world I never would have known. And honestly, I would do it all over again, even if I knew what the outcome would be. I wouldn't trade all the pain and suffering I have endured if it meant I was able to experience the unconditional love of my beautiful child. She is worth it.

The power was within me. I realized I had a choice to make. A choice to live this life feeling sorry for myself or ditch the dark heavy cloak and walk in light. I became determined to find that silver lining, not taking anything for granted, and use my new knowledge and pain to make the most of every day. I was capable of discovering that light in the darkness, and able to be that light for others.

> No, dear brothers and sisters, I have not achieved it,[a] but I focus on this one thing: Forgetting the past and looking forward to what lies ahead, I press on to reach the end of the race and receive the heavenly prize for which God, through Christ Jesus, is calling us (Philippians 3: 13-14).

I have experienced the worst. Sometimes I still relive those gut-wrenching, soul-killing sobs and sharp pains. However, instead of that initial blanket of hopelessness, these intimate moments are followed by an overwhelming peace that embraces me, bringing comfort and healing. This is the gift of grief and God's grace.

I can honestly say that having lived through the trauma of the death of my child, my eyes have been opened to a new world. Initially, it was a world full of unending sadness and pain. It was a world of heavy doubts and perpetual what-ifs.

It's weird and hard to convey in words, a strange phenomenon. At times, I am so overwhelmed with sadness that I have to live without her it's hard to fathom. It wasn't fair, yet I am forever grateful to have had her in my life.

God has let me experience a love like no other. He has given me the gift of being a mother (five times) and the unexpected gift of grief as well. I have experienced the worst yet I have survived and my heart and eyes have been opened to the reality of just how fragile life is and how incredibly deep humans are capable of loving. It's pretty astonishing when you ponder it.

Ten years later, it has evolved into a world of deep introspect and life lessons. Grief is constantly developing and molding my heart of compassion while pruning my spirit and blossoming my faith. Grief causes you to become authentic to yourself as you walk that fine line between past and present, delicately balancing the dynamic emotions that flood your soul, while reflecting on yesterday and pondering what the future holds.

I have learned that I cannot only survive this, but can thrive. It humbles me to know that without grief, my life would have been entirely different and I would not be the same person I have become today. For that I am grateful.

If you're reading this then you know. To be told your beloved child has died is the worst pain. It's a paralyzing and debilitating state that leaves you feeling like you are suffocating, making you scream in terror and disbelief. And this can last for months, even years, as you desperately try to wake up from such a horrifying dream.

My heart is heavy knowing that each day someone new will join this club. It's not fair, this arduous, frightening journey that's forced upon some unsuspecting parents. Tomorrow it will be someone else's father, mother, brother, sister, son, or daughter.

It knows no discrimination. No one is exempt. Loss. Grief. They will find us at some point in our lives when we least expect it, pulling us into an abyss of heartbreak and despair. And then what?

My point: Among the daily stress, tension, and challenges of life, stop and search for gratitude. We must be cognizant of the incredible gifts that have been bestowed upon us. It's a miraculous gift to even be alive, to experience our five senses, to breathe, smell, taste, hear and see. To laugh, cry, walk and love.

So, for that car that is broken, give thanks that you have a car to fix. For that necessary and expensive home repair, give thanks and realize what a gift it is to even have a home. For that taxing job, give thanks that it helps pay the bills. For that exhausting child, give thanks for their strong personality, and recall how wonderful it was the day they were born.

> You will always remember your [loved one],
> and your grief over his death won't go away
> quickly. But in time, your pain will lessen—
> and God wants to help you in this process.
> What can you do? First, take time each day
> to thank God for the years you had together.
> Thankfulness is like a healing balm to
> our souls. ~ Billy Graham

Find perspective. Embrace it. Look with eyes of wonder and hope for tomorrow. Take time to enjoy the rainbow of colors in that sunset, appreciate being able to hear those birds singing or see the wildlife out your window. Smile with joy when you're able to spend time with family and friends, laughing and adoring such wonderful company.

Many of us are clouded by judgment until we, too, experience a rock-bottom tragedy. Daily challenges can be upsetting, but we're fortunate right now to not to be standing where someone else is. For someone who is grieving, they've lost part of themselves. They are left struggling with a gaping hole deep in their soul, an unforgettable void that can never be filled nor replaced.

I suggest embracing gratitude, the healing vessel through grief. Finding and purposefully seeking out the simple beauty of life. Take time to smell those fragrant roses. Make time to read a book, go for a walk, play a game, or admire a sunset. Be cognizant of the smile that comes to your face when you hear your child's name. Grief takes us back to the stone ages with no cellphones or internet, like a time warp of dream lands filled with precious memories and heartache, making us live in hindsight, wishing that we could go back and do things differently.

When my children draw rainbows on the walls with permanent markers, make a complete disaster out of the house, or if I spill my hot chocolate down the front of my clothes while rushing out the door, no matter how upset I feel, I try to embrace these little inconveniences. Now I know that in the grand scheme of things, this is nothing. When I'm overworked, stressed and feel like I can't make it another day, I remember how far I've come, and stand on His promises.

In an instant, we learn what's really important and to appreciate the little things. And you know that saying, don't sweat the small stuff? It couldn't be more true.

Having gratitude ignites the soul and renews the mind. It gives us that wholeness and satisfaction that our hearts desire. Lydia taught me to love unconditionally, believe in myself, have confidence and live each day to the fullest. She was an outgoing, sparkling little girl who nourished my zest for life.

Gratitude possesses immense life-changing power. If you are willing, it can transform your heart and allow you to see the world through an eternal perspective and rose colored glasses.

Intentionally search for that sunshine. Count those blessings. Try to take fifteen minutes each day and write down ten things that you are thankful for.

Here is my journal entry from April 25, 2015:

I feel defeated and the tears start to fall. I retreated into the kitchen after dishing up breakfast for the children when it hits me hard. I open the pantry door and lean in, and sob as my elbow rests on the shelf with my hand on my forehead. I cry out to God, why does this have to be so difficult?

After seeing that picture I hadn't seen in years, I felt a sense of intense need and sadness surround me. I craved her. I desperately need to feel her touch, her presence, her embrace. The thought that I never will again knocked me to my knees. It's a craving that is never satisfied. God is enough. Is he really? At first I wasn't so sure. But I know He will sustain me.

As the day turned to night and beautiful pastels painted the sky, I was so relieved when the children fell asleep. I am so tired and they were so wild. The house was finally quiet. All I can hear are faint breaths by the children, slowly inhaling and exhaling into peaceful slumber. Thank goodness. My little guy, with bright red lips and a sticky face, his long eyelashes twitch as he dreams, is content with no worries. My tears built up waiting for me to allow the faucet to run freely. How could I ever want for more. I am blessed but not worthy. Home is a feeling not a place.

For some incredible articles and websites on grief and gratitude, as well as fabulous gratitude journal prompts, download the Barely Breathing Workbook at DaphneBachGreer.com.

Here's a little snippet I wrote as a co-author for the Amazon bestselling Kindle book, *Everyday Joy*. . .

> She found joy and wonder in every little
> thing. And joy and wonder always found her.
> ~ Katrina Mayer

How much would our lives improve if we acknowledged and appreciated the little things in life? Everyday joy is hearing the deep giggles of a baby, embracing chaos, being mesmerized by the colors of the vibrant summer blooms and captivating sunsets. It brews happiness from within. A friendly smile, silly antics from a pet, a kind gesture from a coworker all bring that emotional fulfillment many of us crave. But life isn't always sunshine and rainbows. To make it through life's struggles, we must uncover the joy buried within, allowing us to transform our struggles into blessings. We must focus, choosing to keep our eyes on the prize. Seeking everyday joy, drives us to be authentic with ourselves, letting seeds of hope and joy reign over our hearts.

It means finding beauty in the moment. Joy replenishes your soul and revives your spirit, igniting your faith and allows you to rest in His peace. Intentionally choosing to recognize the simple gifts in everyday life grants us an eternal perspective which shall not be shaken. It just may be what you've been searching for all along.

Those who sow in tears will reap
with shouts of joy (Psalm 126:5).

> Other people are going to find healing in
> your wounds. Your greatest life messages
> and your most effective ministry will come
> out of your deepest hurts. ~ Rick Warren

SECRET 10

SHARE YOUR JOURNEY

Have you ever shared your journey? Your heartbreak, successes, your most intimate and sacred walks through trials and loss? Whether with complete strangers or a close friend, make that attempt to reach out to others no matter how difficult.

For me, sharing didn't come easy. I'm one of those stuffer kinds, where I shove my feelings and emotions deep down, shielding them from the world. Very private emotionally, I fought this battle for years, keeping silent my pain and sorrow. However, there came a time when I couldn't keep bottling up my feelings.

Gradually, after feeling compelled by God to share my journey via my support groups, blog and books, I began writing more which has resulted in a remarkable transformation in me. It is absolutely apprehensive and scary, yet rewarding and miraculous at the same time. I've made so many new friends and reached deep into the hearts of many that struggled with the same feelings of loss that I had.

Learning from each other is priceless, and planting seeds of hope for others is invaluable.

It wasn't always easy. My first few times verbally sharing my story brought heavy sobs that made it impossible to finish. Sometimes it was hard to write, to put my pain into words. Occasionally, I still shed those tears when telling about our accident and unbelievable journey.

Seeing my words on paper and reading them back has proved to be quite difficult at times, too. To verbalize this dark reality somehow makes it tangible yet, when we do share, our heavy cement boots become just a bit lighter. While we yearn to go back to our previous life when our children were alive, it's so important to be real with yourself, acknowledging where you're at yet awkwardly embracing the strenuous path that awaits.

When we share life events, we become keenly aware that others who are with us have been down a similar path, and we aren't alone after all. Someone else has sobbed in disbelief, succumbed to shock and despair, and experienced the darkest of days just like you have.

When you share your journey, you create connections with other parents who have also experienced the loss of their child, and the pain softens. It's a strange comfort, knowing others understand your pain and are fighting the same battle. By blogging, talking with a friend, sharing in a support group, with counselors, at church or at a retreat, it unites you all and ignites the healing process. Over time, you'll internally recognize that your story gradually evolves from horrific pain and tragic loss to the wonderful qualities and life of your child.

Your eyes will slowly open and one day you'll become vibrantly aware of where you've been, where you're at, and how far you have come. You will find that your capacity to love has grown to infinite levels. You see things differently now, through eyes of compassion. Miraculously and inadvertently, you will slowly heal yourself as you share your journey more and more.

As time goes by, you will gain confidence in telling your story and it will become easier. This is your story. No one else's. It becomes real and becomes a core part of who you are now.

Courageously and confidently, without even knowing it, you may impact others and become a beacon of hope for those who are just beginning down this road of unfathomable pain.

> Without God, life has no purpose, and
> without purpose, life has no meaning.
> Without meaning, life has no significance
> or hope.. ~ Rick Warren

For in this hope we were saved; but hope
that is seen is no hope at all. Who hopes for
what he can already see? But if we hope for
what we do not yet see, we wait for it
patiently (Romans 8:24-25).

BONUS SECRETS

Ten years have passed since my beloved five-year-old little girl went to heaven. That is so hard to believe. Sometimes I feel like it was all a dream, yet it also seems like yesterday, too. Through this time, I have struggled for my life, grappled with my faith, questioned eternity, and fought for my marriage, all while parenting the best I could. Not an easy feat.

Grieving parents are thrust onto an out-of-control rollercoaster, never to get off. Never. That thought alone is terrifying. However, over time, the unpredictable turns will soften, the pace becomes more tolerable, and the highs and lows will feel more manageable.

Blessed am I to be able to share with you all the survival secrets I've learned along the way. And there's not just ten secrets to survival. There is an entire toolbox of survival skills. Yet, I cannot list them all. We all have our own coping mechanisms for how to survive. What works for one doesn't work for all.

Remember, you have been wonderfully and fearfully made. There is no right or wrong way to grieve. However, I can share with you the most influential secrets to surviving this unspeakable loss that I have experienced in my own life as a grieving mother. I sincerely hope these secrets have made an impact on you, and that is has opened your heart to trying new things. You know the first ten, below are a few more.

MEDICATIONS

No one ever told me that grief felt
so much like fear. ~C.S. Lewis

Seeing my five-year-old daughter lying in her hot-pink casket, surrounded by her stuffed animals was more than I could take. Hyperventilating in disbelief, I soon became introduced to anxiety, panic, and depression—grief's best friends. Beware, they will try to sabotage you any chance they get. Your mind is such a powerful thing. Our thoughts race and race, telling us lies that can provoke us into a downward spiral in no time at all.

Are medications the answer? Truth be told, there is no pill to fix grief. While self-medicating with alcohol and drugs can be tempting, they offer only a temporary solution along with potential to increase the pain. Thus, I've found these are not the solution.

How can you handle the wild unpredictable feelings of grief when the pendulum swings out of control with guilt, anger, suicide, nightmares, flashbacks, depression and everything else? By all means, medications are here for a reason. They can be an asset to the broken-hearted and all our accompanying ailments, allowing us to cope. If you are feeling that you just cannot tackle this and day-to-day survival is more than you can bear, make that appointment with your medical provider without fail.

Personally, I did contact my doctor and was grateful for anxiety medications. Without it, I was unable to handle simple things like a busy schedule, loud noises, chaos, meal preparation, parenting and even contentious conversations. I desperately needed a buffer between my mind and my reality. My heart would race, and my breathing would become out of control as panic filled my mind. I only used them a few times over the years, but relied on them to fix me during those difficult times when my mind was not able to function well. There were times I urgently needed them and they did their job, calming my severed heart.

However, years later, I knew I didn't want to be dependent upon a pill to survive this. This internal, soul-crushing pain was something that would last a lifetime. As a result, I gradually transitioned away from medication and learned that God is the only one in control, and the only one I need. His word held the cure for everything I was going through and anything I was feeling. There is a scripture to match it all. Peace, joy and healing, He offered it all. I had reached a benchmark, where I let my medication expire, and turned to His word during those disparaging times, believing in the power of prayer. I carried my Bible everywhere. In my car, my purse, to work, everywhere I went. It gave me a sense of security I couldn't find elsewhere. I relied solely on Him. I trusted Him.

There will be those high peaks and low valleys for sure. However, at some point and time, it may be weeks or decades later, we will need to remove our temporary band-aid, reevaluate our reliance on medications and face our reality, finding a balance in our new normal. It's so important to remember that every person is unique and there is no time limit to your grief, nor a proper way to grieve. Remember, you are not alone and help is just a phone call away.

SELF-CARE

> I have come to believe that caring for myself
> is not self-indulgent. Caring for myself is an
> act of survival. ~ Audre Lorde

This quote speaks volumes. Child loss becomes an act of survival. As we sift through the shock and trauma, we must remember to take care of ourselves during this fragile time.

Be gentle with yourself. You have experienced more trauma than many will experience in their lifetime. Worry, anxiety, depression, aches and pains will come your way. You child has died. Your future has been shattered. This is a lot for your brain to process. Physically and emotionally our bodies and minds take a toll. Grief brain is a real thing. Our thoughts are scrambled, sometimes irrational and our memory has left us for the most part. And that's okay. Impossible days will arrive. Be patient with yourself. It takes time. Rampant and unpredictable emotions will do their best to overwhelm you. So make sure to take time for you. Remember, it's okay to say no. It's okay to stay, to not leave your home and it's okay to keep busy. It's all up to you. You can't rush the grieving process.

It's so easy to put ourselves on the backburner, as all our energy is used on grieving. Remember to take care of yourself and embrace breaks from your emotions. Try to keep cognizant of your own needs, physical, emotional and spiritual. Keep those dental appointments, medical checkups, and stay hydrated. And of course, do something you enjoy. Try to eat. Try to rest. Try to identify calming activities that help you relax. And do more of them. Moderation is key. Be gentle with yourself and welcome help from others.

NUTRITION & EXERCISE

> Take care of your body. It's the only
> place you have to live. ~ Jim Rohn

When our child dies, we are thrown into a foreign world full of shock and disbelief; the last thing on our mind is to exercise and eat properly. After Lydia died, my house overflowed with flowers and an abundance of food, casseroles—you name it we had it. The refrigerator had never been so full. Our gracious law enforcement community organized an entire month's worth of meals for us, so we didn't have to cook for weeks! This was incredible, a lifesaver, as we couldn't take care of ourselves and were barely able to care for our young son. For four weeks, a different law enforcement agency each week, would prepare meals and deliver them to us. From casseroles to pizza, pies and cakes, breakfast, they covered it all. The compassion we felt was overwhelming.

But what about when all that goes away, or if you don't have that luxury? When we are deep in grief, the last thing we think about is food and nutrition. You don't want to cook, and you don't want to eat. Your mind may even play tricks on you, making you think you don't deserve to eat since your child will not be eating with you. The power of the mind is incredible.

Weight slipped off me gradually as I lost about ten pounds after Lydia died. I had no appetite despite all the food in my home. I remember people constantly trying to get me to eat for days. I didn't want to and didn't care if I never ate again.

Eating healthy wasn't something I cared about. I was fine with ice cream for breakfast, lunch and dinner. However, I know that fueling our bodies is essential for sustaining good physical and mental health. Keeping that balanced diet full of nutritious foods, vitamins and minerals can be a challenge when you're in deep grief. Grieving your child is hard on your body physically. Incredibly hard. That's why it's so important to try to eat as well as you can to keep yourself healthy during this unfathomable time.

Do the best you can. Try to maintain a healthy diet and get your body moving.

I may not be the best one to speak about exercise, because I love to eat and flop on the couch as much as the next person. However, I do find enjoyment and solace out when I'm out hunting and hiking in nature. I feel a strong connection there that revives my spirit and brings me peace.

It's no secret that exercise is good for you. Some find that exercise is the key to coping with grief. When life feels so out of control, exercise and nutrition are things you can control. It renews the spirit, gives you energy while cleansing your soul, encourages healthy breathing and refreshes your mind. It releases stress and reignites your physical body, resulting in a calming and relaxing state. We can all regulate our activity and do as much or little as we like.

What types of exercise can you do? Anything that appeals to you such as nature walks, going to the gym, walking with a friend, swimming, walking the dog, yoga and so much more.

> There are no quick fixes to grief. No easy answers. Every expression of grief that wants to be felt and honored and give its space must be allowed in order to heal.
> ~ Tom Zuba

COUNSELING

Whether to seek outside help with your grief is something many grapple with. The million dollar question—go to counseling or not? We are all different and our capabilities to handle stress and tragedy are innately different. In my experience, counseling helps you cope with this unbearable new journey. Especially in those early months and years, experiencing the death of your child is a giant monster we can't combat alone. Finding someone to guide and assist you as you navigate the pain can be a key part of the healing process.

It's difficult enough to manage yourself when you're grieving your child, it's important to be aware that child loss also conjures up difficulties in other aspects of your life including marriage, work, finances, family and other relationships. Again, we are all different and grief is unique to every individual. What works for one, may not work for another. On that note, there is no right or wrong time to start counseling. It's entirely up to what feels best for you.

Personally, I always considered myself someone who could handle it all. Anything and everything life threw at me. I was so strong and raised to be that way. Yet when my daughter died suddenly, I was lost and knew I couldn't do this on my own.

I was eager to see my counselor who had become a Godsend. Initially, in my clouded state of mind, I believed she would have some magical dust or tricks to rid me of my suffering. I was a tough girl, able to comfortably discuss anything that came my way, but this was something I had no idea how to tackle and was terrified to face.

She wanted to hear about her. She asked me about my daughter. The wall I had started to build gently began to shake and fall in the wake of her interest and genuine curiosity. It was comforting to sit with someone who wanted to hear about my daughter, to hear me talk about my precious girl and allow me to share my love for her, rather than always avoiding the elephant in the room.

For the first few appointments, I sat on the loveseat in my counselor's office, my feet curled under me, my head hung low, sobbing, tears falling from my cheeks, unable to mutter a word. She would glance toward me, but words eluded me. The elephant in the room was sitting on me. How could I ignore it? I couldn't tell her specifics of the accident or much else. I didn't remember them all, and some were too difficult to utter. Either way, did it matter? Lydia was gone. Finally, I said, "I just wish I could fast-forward six months."

I wanted so badly to know I was going to be okay, and that time would rescue me from this horrible pain.

Her eyes still on me, and compassion encompassing her very being, she responded by telling me that it took on average two to five years to even come to terms with the death of a child. I almost fell out of my chair. The weight of her words crushed me, as fear and despair gripped my soul even tighter. It had not quite been a month since the accident. How was I supposed to get through years? Every part of me became weaker, and I no longer wanted see the future, wondering if there could even be a future for me. This was more than I could bear.

I considered her response. Years? Two to five years just to come to terms with Lydia's death? Would I ever feel peace again? Would life ever feel good again? Was it worth it? Was it even possible to live under such a cloud of pain, shame, and unrelenting agony?

In all reality, I attended counseling regularly for five years. Five years. Yep, that's right. That sounds like a long time, and yet it passed by incredibly fast. She was a refreshing soul and someone who could really understand me. Although I sat quietly during many sessions, she offered words that resonated within me. She discussed her concern for my physical and mental health as I sat curled up in a ball of guilt and shame. I eagerly anticipated our visits and realized what a blessing she was to me.

Through the years, my counselor became my biggest advocate and encourager, a true healing vessel through the raging river of grief.

I believe we absolutely need that extra support and a professional perspective, someone to guide us when our minds are not our own. Someone we can trust, someone who will listen. There are many grief counselors, coaches, online programs and support out there. Please reach out and contact one if you're stuck or have difficulties navigating your way through the loss of your child. You have nothing to lose, and it just may be the best decision of your life.

> Music gives a soul to the universe,
> wings to the mind, flight to the
> imagination and life to everything.
> ~ Plato

MUSIC

What a gift music can be. Music is prevalent in most of our lives. We listen to it in our cars, in shopping malls, on television, on the radio and our cellphones, and many other places. We download our favorite songs and move to the rhythm, reciting lyrics effortlessly.

Music was something I intentionally avoided for the first several months after Lydia died. I dreaded the radio coming on or hearing songs on the television. Every tune brought a fresh wave of pain. Every type—love songs, joyful songs, sad songs, energetic songs—held me captive, reminding me of the absence of my daughter, causing a downward spiral of wailing and endless tears. At the time, my guilt was weighing down on me and I couldn't bear to listen to any music.

Music reaches the soul and penetrates us on the deepest level, allowing an outlet for those darkest emotions causing them to emerge to the surface. It connects us to our spiritual self while verbalizing our thoughts and feelings. It is so immensely powerful. Music can also be frightening and something grieving parents avoid because we know it will bring incessant tears, making us acutely aware of situations that could cause instant facial waterfalls. Yet we also can use music as a distraction, which empowers us to manage that soul-scarring uncertainty. However, when we face that music, it can purify the heart, revealing our endless love and release our hurt.

For some, it becomes a catalyst for healing and for feeling. As time progressed, I found that church hymns and uplifting music became particularly therapeutic for me. This type of music moved me like nothing else. Oftentimes, while sitting in the back row pew at Sunday service, I am transformed into a world of wetness when the music starts and my eyes began to weep. Those lyrics are so real, piercing the core of my being. At times, I'm not able to stop the tears, yet ironically, this is when I feel closest to God. Music makes me feel real. It provides perspective. I get goosebumps and feel His presence and eternal hope when songs of praise arrive at my ears. What a beautiful blessing music can be.

> Music expresses that which cannot
> be put into words. ~ Victor Hugo

I'm not a medical provider. I'm just a mom who has lived through the unimaginable. These tips are not here to try to fix you or make you happy, but to give you some tools on surviving. Despite all odds, it can be done.

Again, you don't have to do this alone. Go back to the ten secrets, reread and reevaluate them. Take action on those you've put off no matter how uncomfortable or scary. Most importantly, remember that this life is nothing compared to the eternity that awaits us.

Keep an eternal perspective. Remember one day at a time. You can do this!

And there you have it. Treasured secrets learned by a mother's tragedy. Don't give up. Love always wins.

When you are sorrowful, look again in your
heart, and you shall see that in truth you
are weeping for that which has been
your delight. ~ Khalil Gibran

CONCLUSION

I don't have all the answers. I just know what has worked for me, and want to share those tools with you.

Broken souls, we are.

That unpleasant feeling that arises when we see people happy and smiling when our child has just died is like getting punched in the gut. Don't they get it? Don't they understand what you're going through? Honestly? No. They don't get it. Secretly, we long for their comfort yet never wish them the same pain. It's a fragile walk. We must talk about our grief, and quit dancing around the elephant in the room with people who just don't understand.

And as we wonder where God is in all this mess, let's try to live with an eternal perspective, remembering that His promises are rock solid. His faithfulness never ceases nor should it be questioned. Take time to study the word and pray. Cry out to Him, scream, whisper or sob with Him. Remember, He sees what's in your heart.

Seek those comforting scriptures and learn about those disciples and people in the Bible who ultimately kept their faith and endured the struggles in life's storms.

Losing a child rips apart your inner core, crushing your spirit and soul. It ravages the very foundation of who you are, and replaces it with a new identity you didn't ask for. It's not an easy road.

No matter what anyone tells you, grief doesn't fit into neat stages. It's messy, unpredictable rollercoasters of emotions that collide when we least expect it. But let me reassure you—you can learn to ride those waves of grief while progressing forward. You will have good days and you will have ugly, bad days. But no matter how hopeless it seems, in the end, you will prevail.

We are resilient beings. You can achieve peace and happiness, while still honoring and remembering your child.

> May the God of hope fill you with all joy and peace as you trust in him, so that you may overflow with hope by the power of the Holy Spirit (Romans 15:13).

He has called us to be bold and courageous. Time will reveal the blessings of hindsight and perspective. We are anointed to move more boldly and live without fear, for we have been through the worst. We are equipped and can step out in faith, not waffling nor worrying about what others think or what the future may hold. We got this.

No matter the age of our child when they passed away, no matter how they died, it doesn't matter. Remember to appreciate those little things. I find gratitude in Lydia's hot pink nail polish stain she left on our white carpet, the boogers she wiped above her headboard on the wall, the shoe pile in the middle of the floor, the beautiful flowers in bloom and the beauty of nature. Marvel at how far you've come. Never forget that tomorrow is not promised and every day is a gift.

I am so thankful God allowed me to be her mother, even if it was only for a short time. To fall down laughing during Ring-Around-the-Rosie, to do makeup and play dress-up, take part in endless board games and jumping in the fall leaves, what a gift I have been given. She taught me the ultimate lessons about faith and love. We may not get to watch them grow older, yet we were chosen to be their parents. A unbreakable bond created to last until eternity.

After experiencing the worst possible tragedy in life, all my hope was shattered that first year. My preconceived notions of what hope meant was tossed out the window when my daughter died, shattering my expectations for any type of future. Life as I knew it had ended.

As if stepping outside my own body, I was instantly transformed into someone I didn't know. I had become a stranger who was living a life that was unraveling at an alarming rate. I felt like a helpless kitten tangled in an enormous ball of yarn that was becoming more and more disarrayed. Daily tasks like cooking, bathing, and even getting a drink of water required too much effort. Each time I actually accomplished something, it felt like a major milestone.

Things like this didn't happen to people like me. I had naively believed this, but they do. And it did.

I couldn't rationalize what had taken place, and I began to despise the phrase, "Bad things happen to good people." It wasn't fair, and I was struggling just to breathe.

Slowly, as the days and months progressed, glimmers of hope were planted inside me. I recognized that Lydia wouldn't want me to be sad forever. I started to appreciate life, recognizing the fragility of this brief stay on earth and began to see the beauty in ordinary things. I found myself appreciating the sunrise and the majestic rainbow of colors in the sunset, studying the intricacy of insects and animals, and being thankful for having a roof over my head. I appreciated those arguments with my children, the piles of laundry and toys scattered around the house. Little things became big things.

I no longer expected and waited for tragedy to strike me again. I would hear about many others who were struggling much more than I. My soul felt their pain, and I was humbled. My heart became full of compassion and love for others who were experiencing hardships, giving me an incredible urge to live my life differently than how I had lived so many years before. This life was no longer about me, but about what I could do for others.

Hope had arrived. It had miraculously floated in on a drop of dew one cold spring morning and landed in my lap, leaving a lasting impression upon me. Little by little I recognized just how blessed I really was. Hope is having a positive outlook on life and not taking anything for granted. We don't have to live in the past. Conversely, we need to live this fleeting life expecting incredible things to happen. Praying, giving, receiving joyfully and having a heart full of gratitude can transform your life in ways never imagined. Amidst the darkness, there is always hope.

As I wrote in Amazon's number one bestseller, *Success Is Yours*, experiencing heartbreak and loss can shatter your soul and leave you inundated with grief, feeling lost and alone with no hope in sight. Is it possible to find joy again? Absolutely! You can thrive once again.

I was an average suburban mom who loved her daughter. When she died, I didn't believe it was feasible to smile again. Yet, I am proof that anything is possible.

How can you achieve it? Embrace faith. Take one day at a time. Be patient.

It requires clinging to hope and believing in an entity bigger than you. It's trusting that there is more to life than just this world. It takes opening your heart and blessing others, giving, serving and loving while gradually rebuilding your life. As you discover your purpose and passion, embrace your hurt and treasure your memories. Honor your past, and know you are not alone.

Hope is more powerful than fear. Living intentionally and connecting with others will surely reignite your spirit and transform your heart like you could never imagine. Reclaim your life and become determined to restore your happiness. Persevere, and never give up. If

I can do it, so can you! Remember, be easy with yourself. You're doing the best you can.

And now, I take a deep breath and silently give thanks for the love of Christ and all the blessings he has bestowed upon me. His mercy, His grace, His strength, His love, His forgiveness and the gift of salvation. And then I hand it all over to him and recognize that God's got this.

> I can do ALL things, through Christ who
> gives me strength (Philippians 4:13).

I am on this journey with you...

> And when great souls die, after a period
> peace blooms, slowly and always irregularly.
> Spaces fill with a kind of soothing electric
> vibration. Our senses, restored, never to be
> the same, whisper to us. They existed. They
> existed. We can be. Be and be better. For
> they existed. ~ Maya Angelou

APPENDIX

Ellie's Way   elliesway.org
Ellie's Way mission is to organize, maximize, and deliver assistance to
people affected by tragedy.

While We're Waiting   whilewerewaiting.org
Faith-based retreats for bereaved parents.

Grief Share.   griefshare.org
Faith-based grief program

The Compassionate Friends   CompassionateFriends.org

Grieving Mothers   Facebook.com/grievingmother

Grieving Dads   grievingdads.com

Grieving Parents Support Network   grievingparents.net

A Bed for My Heart   abedformyheart.com

Bereaved Parents of the USA   bereavedparentsusa.org

Grief Diaries   griefdiaries.com

Sophie Kinsella   sophiekinsella.co.uk

The Bible   bible.com

Lydia's Love   lydiaslove.org

THANK YOU

I cannot express the wealth of gratitude I have for those who stood by me during the tragic loss of my precious Lydia. My parents and brother, compassionate coworkers, the chaplains who stayed by our side for weeks, the dispatchers, police officers, nurses, doctors, funeral directors, and my sister-in-law and mother-in-law for dressing my princess, and lovingly doing her hair and nails to make her sparkle one more time. They handled all those last details I couldn't even begin to do.

I must offer my sincere appreciation to those few close friends who never gave up on me, always encouraging and believing in me. Without you I wouldn't have made it this far. My new friends, my compassionate friends, you have left a lasting impact more than you know. You make all the difference.

Thank you to my husband Jake and beloved children, Hunter, Andrew, Sadie and John for your patience and opening your hearts, keeping that tender dialogue open and loving me on those days when I'm hardly loveable.

For my heavenly father, thank you for giving me strength and your gift of salvation, for your unconditional love and forgiveness to renew my spirit, allowing me to live your purpose. Thank you for restoring me and opening my eyes, giving me a new life full of compassion and meaning and the gift of seeing an eternal perspective.

DAPHNE BACH GREER

Lydia's mom

ABOUT

DAPHNE BACH GREER

Daphne Greer is a native of eastern Oregon, where she continues to reside with her husband, Jake, and their four living children. She enjoys the country lifestyle and love for the outdoors. She has worked in the criminal justice field for nearly twenty years as an adult probation and parole officer.

Following the death of her daughter in 2008, Daphne found a new purpose and passion in life. She cofounded Lydia's Love, a nonprofit organization that provides birthday celebrations to children in need.

She blogs at grievinggumdrops.com and writes about finding hope amidst grief and loss. She is a member of the Oregon Christian Writers Association, and also served for many years on the steering committee of The Compassionate Friends in Salem, Oregon. Currently, Daphne volunteers with Ellie's Way, a nonprofit organization proving hope and outreach for the bereaved as well as While We're Waiting, a faith-based organization providing retreats for bereaved parents.

She is coauthor of *Grief Diaries: Will We Survive*, and the Amazon bestsellers *Success is Yours*, *Everyday Joy*, *A Gift of Gratitude*, and *What We Love*. She has contributed to many other books and websites sharing her journey and experience on finding hope through loss.

Please join her at grievinggumdrops.com or DaphneBachGreer.com to get the Barely Breathing Workbook, or to connect and share. She would love to hear from you. You may also reach her by email at daphnebgreer@gmail.com.

DAPHNE BACH GREER
FINDING FAITH ♥ RESTORING LIFE ♥ IGNITING HOPE

ALYBLUE MEDIA TITLES

Faces of Resilience
Faith, Grief & Pass the Chocolate Pudding
Grief Diaries: Surviving Sudden Loss
Grief Diaries: Surviving Loss by Cancer
Grief Diaries: Victim Impact Statement
Grief Diaries: Hit by Impaired Driver
Grief Diaries: Surviving Loss of a Spouse
Grief Diaries: Surviving Loss of a Child
Grief Diaries: Surviving Loss of a Sibling
Grief Diaries: Surviving Loss of a Parent
Grief Diaries: Surviving Loss of an Infant
Grief Diaries: Surviving Loss of a Loved One
Grief Diaries: Surviving Loss by Suicide
Grief Diaries: Surviving Loss of Health
Grief Diaries: How to Help the Newly Bereaved
Grief Diaries: Loss by Impaired Driving
Grief Diaries: Loss by Homicide
Grief Diaries: Loss of a Pregnancy
Grief Diaries: Hello from Heaven
Grief Diaries: Grieving for the Living
Grief Diaries: Shattered
Grief Diaries: Project Cold Case
Grief Diaries: Poetry & Prose and More
Grief Diaries: Through the Eyes of Men
Grief Diaries: Will We Survive?
Real Life Diaries: Living with a Brain Injury
Real Life Diaries: Through the Eyes of DID
Real Life Diaries: Through the Eyes of an Eating Disorder
Real Life Diaries: Living with Endometriosis
Real Life Diaries: Living with Mental Illness
Real Life Diaries: Living with Rheumatic Disease
Real Life Diaries: Through the Eyes of a Funeral Director
Real Life Diaries: Living with Gastroparesis
My Grief Diary
Grammy Visits From Heaven
Grandpa Visits From Heaven
Heaven Talks to Children
Color My Soul Whole
A Child is Missing: A True Story
A Child is Missing: Searching for Justice

Humanity's legacy of stories and storytelling
is the most precious we have.

~ DORIS LESSING

PUBLISHED BY ALYBLUE MEDIA
Real stories. Real people. Real hope.
www.AlyBlueMedia.com

Made in the USA
San Bernardino, CA
07 July 2020

75068800R00078